Out of the Cloister

Out of the Cloister

A Study of Organizational Dilemmas

Helen Rose Fuchs Ebaugh

seminary library
Charles L. Souvay Memorial

University of Texas Press Austin & London

Library of Congress Cataloging in Publication Data

Ebaugh, Helen Rose Fuchs, 1942–
    Out of the cloister.

    Bibliography: p.
    1. Monasticism and religious orders for women.
I. Title.
BX4200.E25   255'.9   76-54503
ISBN 0-292-76007-8

The publication of this book was assisted by a
grant from the Andrew W. Mellon Foundation.

For Albert L. Ebaugh, M.D.,

my husband and best friend

Contents

Tables

Figures

Preface

Out of the Cloister is a book about nuns, nuns in the aggregate known as religious orders or convents and nuns as individual women faced with very human decisions. Woven throughout the book as an interpretative thread is also an autobiography, since I am convinced that the book would have been impossible without my ten years' experience as a Catholic nun. On all three levels—organizationally, in terms of individual women, and autobiographically—there has been a movement in the past fifteen years away from a cloistered, enclosed way of life toward a more open and socially involved existence. This book analyzes that movement from historical, sociological, and social psychological perspectives.

Because the book is not written in the first person and because I was as scientifically objective as possible in the collection and interpretation of data, I feel I owe the reader some explication of how my personal life influenced the research process. I offer these introductory remarks not primarily for the purpose of human interest. My main purpose is to reflect and delineate some of the ways in which personal biography influences a researcher's choice of subject matter and manner of approaching and interpreting data.

In his article "Insiders and Outsiders," Robert K. Merton focuses upon the unique perspectives brought to research situations by insiders, that is, persons who are part of what they study, and, in contrast, by outsiders, who stand outside the situation they are analyzing.[1] Merton suggests that insiders and outsiders should unite in their intellectual pursuits so that the advantages of each position can be maximized.

When Merton wrote the final draft of that article I was both a student of his and a Catholic nun about to begin a dissertation on the increasing exodus of women from religious orders. I had no intention at the time of leaving the order. Whether by fate or by coincidence, I ended up collecting data as an insider and analyzing it as an outsider. While not consciously related to my research interests, the timing of my decision to leave proved advantageous.

As an insider, the fact that I was a nun during the years 1963–1973 was very helpful because in those ten years religious orders underwent tremendous changes. I became a nun at a time when the old order still persisted even though the breezes from Pope John XXIII's era of renewal and reform had just begun to be felt. We still wore the eighteenth century habit, including bonnet, veil, waist-length cape, and flowing skirt adorned with wooden cross and rosary beads. We gave up the names we had since birth and took on new names given us by a superior. The three vows of poverty, chastity, and obedience had not yet been reinterpreted as communal sharing, celibacy, and openness to the spirit. The voice of the superior had a divine ring, for we were taught that God made his desires known through every command and suggestion of superiors.

However, during my year of strict introduction to the order as a novice, along with the existing constitution and customs of the order we read and discussed such forward-looking books as *The Nun in the World*.[2] During that year also the pope and bishops were gathered in Rome for the Second Vatican Council, which would result in a decree bringing far-reaching changes into religious orders. We were told repeatedly that changes were coming and that we would be in the forefront of determining and implementing them.

During the years 1966–1970 changes did occur very rapidly in many orders. The nature of these changes and their consequences will be discussed in detail throughout this book. At this point, I simply want to emphasize that I was very much involved in the change process, both within my own order and in various other orders throughout the United States. As a young nun with some experience in research, I was one of those in our order who designed and carried out the many self-studies and evaluation programs involved in the reform and renewal efforts. Later on, as a Ph.D. candidate at Columbia University with a specialization in the sociology of religious institutions, I was a consultant to several orders which were agonizing through the struggles of change.

By staying in the order until mid-1973, I also had opportunity to experience the changes that had been made. By then, nuns wore contemporary lay clothes, kept their own names, had much more freedom to choose jobs and living situations, mingled freely in lay society, and were encouraged to exercise individual initiative and responsibility.

My decision to leave the order in the spring of 1973 was not consciously related to the data I had collected on religious orders even though I had interviewed about sixty women who had left three different orders. To what extent my research experience influenced me subconsciously is impossible to determine. No doubt, what I had learned about religious orders from the national survey of orders I had conducted, from three case studies of orders, and from interviews with both nuns and former nuns provided me with evidence that played a part in my decision. However, that decision was a very personal one. Even though, after I left the order, I had several requests from popular magazines to write articles on why I had left and what public statement I intended to make by my leaving, I refused the requests on the ground that my decision was private and unrelated to facts I had discovered and conclusions I had reached because of my research findings.

Whatever the link between my personal life and professional research interests, the fact remains that my sequential insider-outsider roles gave me unique opportunities and perspectives on the institution I was studying. Being an insider was critical not only in obtaining data but also in interpreting it. Many outsiders, including sociologists and psychologists, had previously tried to gain entry into religious orders for research purposes but were turned away precisely because they were seen as intruders. Privacy and secrecy have an important function in religious orders; they serve to isolate members from the larger society and give them a sense of privileged status. Until recent years empirical research was seen as not only useless but harmful since it focuses upon human factors and explains reality apart from divine intervention.

By 1970 many religious orders had conducted self-studies and were somewhat less fearful and more understanding of the limited claims of research. However, being a nun was by far my greatest asset in gaining the cooperation of administrators of orders throughout the United States. I am convinced that the high response rate to the questionnaire I mailed to U.S. orders was largely due to my being an insider. While it is highly probable, in retrospect, that my being a nun made it easier for administrators of religious orders to trust and accept me and the research I was about, I want to assure those who cooperated that I had no idea at the time that I would be leaving my own order within a few years. There was no deception involved in my requesting entrée and cooperation. One of the reasons for this book is to fulfill a responsibility I feel I owe religious superiors and orders that cooperated. I hope that those who provided the basic data for the book will find my presentation of facts accurate and my treatment of the data respectful. In addition, I hope that some orders will find this book helpful in the ongoing process of self-examination and renewal.

My being an insider gave me an advantage in gaining entrée into religious orders. Equally important, it affected the issue of what to study once entrée and permission had been obtained. Most sociologists would have been attuned to the basic organizational and structural aspects of religious orders. However, the unique features of these institutions, the spirit that pervades them and motivates members to belong, might well have been overlooked by someone who had not experienced life as an insider. It is precisely these indefinable yet central aspects that members find most difficult to articulate and explain to one who is not part of the institution. Being an insider is an asset, perhaps an indispensable one, in knowing the right questions to ask in order to get at the important answers.

In like manner, interpretation of data is aided by an insider perspective. For example, why are some nuns upset because their order has lost canonical status in the church or their policy board has ruled that nuns are no longer obligated to wear a veil? Issues that may appear quite trivial or at least insignificant to an outsider may well constitute crises for members of the order.

The advantages of my insider role during the data-collecting process can be summarized in terms of easy entrée, having a feel for the important issues to be researched, and being able to empathize and interpret data from the perspective of those who belong. The concomitant disadvantage I faced as an insider was the danger of losing objectivity, of being so immersed in my data as to lose sociological perspective. As an insider, I had to exercise constant discipline to remain objective. Once I left the order I found it much easier to subject the empirical data to rigorous sociological analysis. It was as though I had undergone a psychological shift and begun to step out of the data and hold them at arm's length. At that point, it became easier to see religious orders as one kind of human institution and to bring sociological theory and perspectives to bear.

For those of you who are not familiar with the organization of the Catholic Church and who are not quite sure exactly what being a nun means, here are a few definitions. A religious order refers to a group of men or women who have been accepted as members into an organization recognized formally by the government of the Catholic Church with the purpose of dedicating their lives to worshiping God and serving the church. There are two types of religious orders: contemplative orders and active orders. In contemplative orders the members spend their days in prayer and meditation with virtually no contact with outsiders. In active orders the members engage in a variety of services to people, such as teaching, social work, and nursing. Strictly speaking, a "nun" is a member of a contemplative order, and a Catholic "sister" belongs to an active order. However, in common parlance all women who belong to religious orders are called nuns. In this book the term *nun* refers to members of active orders.

The challenge of this book is to maximize what I learned about religious orders from both the insider and outsider perspectives. I hope in the pages which follow I can hold on to and share what a celibate life in the Catholic Church means to members while simultaneously analyzing this life-style from the more objective, sociological stance that I now have.

In addition to the challenge of a balanced insider-outsider perspective, I face another challenge in this book: to present data and interpretations of data from the stance of one who lived a satisfying and happy life for ten years as a nun and who is now living a fulfilled and contented life as a married woman. Unlike many ex-nuns, I had the good fortune to leave the order with almost no anger or bitterness. Although I realized that I no longer wanted to remain a nun, I left with very few regrets for my ten years in the order. In fact, I value the experience, especially the human values and discipline it taught me. While it is no longer viable for me, I know that there are many women for whom life in a religious order remains a viable and desirable life-style. One among these is my own sister. I hope this attitude of genuine respect and acceptance is manifest in the pages that follow.

Acknowledgments

Many people helped me write this book. I am grateful to the presidents of religious orders who cooperated in giving me organizational data and who provided lists of former nuns. To those women, in and out of orders, who spent hours talking to me about their experiences I owe special thanks. In many ways, they provided the insights that helped me interpret the story hidden in the organizational statistics.

Professor Paul Ritterband has put more tedious hours into this book than I dare tally. From the time I first conceived the idea of conducting a sociological study of religious orders to the last draft of the manuscript, he provided suggestions and raised many questions that necessitated my exploring the data from new perspectives. His encouragement kept me plodding on in moments when I felt I was drowning in material. Professor Robert K. Merton has had profound influence on my thinking, both as a stimulating teacher and during conversations with him about the changes occurring in religious orders. His way of musing about an issue and raising intriguing questions helped me formulate some of the theoretical aspects of the study. Professors Benjamin Zablocki, Harriet Zuckerman, Gillian Lindt Gollin, and Joseph Fitzpatrick, S.J., gave me helpful comments.

Several of my colleagues at the University of Houston have been invaluable in critiquing the manuscript and suggesting ways of improving it. Janet Chafetz challenged me to consider the changes among Catholic nuns as part of the overall women's movement. In addition, her interest in the study and her reading of the manuscript led to some important revisions. Russell Curtis read the manuscript for its organizational implications and insisted that I emphasize the interplay of organizational and individual data. Harold A. Nelson also suggested some additions to the organizational approach. Michael Grimes and Rodolphe Charest assisted me with computer-related problems.

Jill Alsup helped me construct the organizational survey and get it mailed to religious orders. I remember that we mailed the final ones from Hell's Half Acre, Wyoming. She also assisted me with the interviewing of nuns and ex-nuns. My parents and siblings (all five of them) as well as my close friends, Barbara and Nelson Brown, were very encouraging throughout the process.

At the time the initial data were collected, I was a member of the Sisters of Divine Providence, San Antonio, Texas. The president of the order was very supportive of my research endeavors. Some of the financial support for the study was provided by Our Lady of the Lake College as well as by a small research grant from Columbia University.

By the time I met my husband in Hermann Park, I had analyzed the data and was just beginning to write the book. He and my two step-sons, Nelson and James, have a way of making life fun, even the ordeal of writing a book.

Introduction

Prior to 1960, nuns, cloisters, and convent walls aroused people's curiosity and stirred their imagination because of the secrecy and mysterious aura that surrounded them. Books like Kathryn Hulme's *The Nun's Story*[1] depicted a medieval institution where iron gates clanked shut to keep nuns in and the world out. Exactly what went on inside those gates was left to novelists or fantasy.

During the decade of the sixties, religious orders experienced rapid and far-reaching changes, especially in the area of greater contact with outsiders. Nuns were allowed more freedom to participate in society through personal contacts, and the mass media were given greater access to what was going on within the cloister. While it was now possible to learn what had been happening for the past hundred years in some aspects of convent life, no one inside or outside the convent was quite sure just where the present changes would lead religious orders in the future. The rapidity of the changes and the unrest they were causing made it difficult during those years to have perspective, especially in terms of the long-range consequences for religious orders.

By 1970, things were beginning to settle down, and it became feasible to step back again and survey what had occurred. The media had exposed much of the mystique and drama of convent life. However, those of us who were interested in exploring more systematically the change process and its consequences were left with many weighty questions, questions of interest not just to policy makers within religious orders but also to sociologists and social psychologists interested in the causes and effects of change upon organizations and the people in them.

One of the basic questions I pondered in the spring of 1971 was the very issue of what effect the loss of secrecy and mystery would have on orders. Would women continue to be drawn to these institutions once the drama and "set apartness" of this way of life diminished? What rewards and organizational pulls would keep members and draw new ones? One of my hunches was that the mystery and secrecy of life in an order provided status to Catholic girls and constituted a reward for belonging.

Many other questions were on my mind that spring as I began to consider the possibility of a study on religious orders. What made it possible for a closed, hierarchically structured, tradition-bound institution to respond so rapidly and radically to change? Where did the impetus for change really begin? How were members readied for change? What theological and sociological developments early in the process made such widespread social change possible? What historical factors preceding the decade of the 1960's set the stage for change? Was Vatican Council II in the Catholic Church the paramount change agent, or were seeds of change planted by lower level administrators and among the members themselves? What effects, anticipated and unanticipated, had change had on individual orders as well as on the larger church? These were some of the organizational questions I kept pondering.

At the same time, my professors and peers at Columbia kept raising similar queries. My own membership in a religious order was public knowledge even though I no longer wore distinctive garb. Professors Robert K. Merton, Paul Ritterband, Harriet Zuckerman, Amitai Etzioni, and Theodore Caplow were among those who were very much interested in what was happening within religious orders and who encouraged me to do an intensive organizational study of the process and impact of the changes going on.

In addition to changes in dress, customs, and organizational structures, there was another phenomenon occurring in religious orders during the sixties, one which was much emphasized by the public press—namely, the increasing exodus of nuns from their orders. As an insider who had an opportunity to talk with administrators across the country, I knew that this phenomenon was of great concern to many orders. There was much speculation among nuns and laity alike as to the causes. Some felt that it was the liberal, rapidly changing orders that were losing members. Usually, the advocates of this view could name an order or two in support of their position. Others maintained that the conservative, change-resistant orders were the ones losing most nuns. There seemed to be instances to support this view also. After hearing a number of such debates, I began to wonder just what relationship did exist between organizational change and membership losses. Were nuns leaving because of change or lack of it in their orders? Which kinds of orders were in fact losing more members? Was there a pattern and, if so, what might explain the relationship?

These questions had ramifications beyond just curiosity and personal interest. The issue of membership commitment in organizations was an area where little sociological research had been conducted. Etzioni had made some predictions about the kinds of rewards that were effective in normative institutions.[2] However, very little empirical research was available, especially any considering commitment during periods of rapid organizational change.

In addition, there was very little organizational literature dealing with the processes involved in dissolving or disbanding formal organizations. Yet I realized that some orders were losing members so rapidly that they were virtually going out of existence in the span of a few years.

On another level, there was the question of just who was leaving and why. Was it only young people, who still had family and job options outside the order? Was it the nuns who were sent to school and who came back with questioning and critical minds? Or was it the uneducated, who found it hard to comprehend the changes and were frightened by increased demands for professionalization in the order? *Why* were nuns leaving? What reasons did they themselves articulate for their decision to leave?

I knew there was only one way to find answers and that my dual role as nun-sociologist put me in an ideal position to uncover them. So in the late spring of 1971 I designed a research project which I hoped would result in some answers to these questions.

The kinds of questions I was asking necessitated research on two levels, both organizationally in terms of institutional data on religious orders themselves and then personally in terms of a focus upon individuals who had left. My basic design consisted of three stages:

> 1. A mail survey to every religious order of women in the United States, with emphasis upon organizational data, including the number who had left each year during the 1960's and questions regarding the degree of change in the order.
> 2. Case studies of three orders, each at a different stage in the change process—a change-oriented order, a change-resistant order, and a middle-of-the-road order regarding degree of change.
> 3. Interviews with women who had left each of the three case study orders.

In early summer of 1971 I sent out the mail questionnaires. I hoped for a 30 percent response rate or, in my optimistic moments, 40 percent. I was overwhelmed by the 67 percent response rate I finally obtained. In the latter part of the summer and early fall I conducted the case studies and interviewed ex-nuns from the three orders. Again, cooperation on the part of these interviewees was very positive.

Before presenting the actual data that resulted from the three-stage research process, there are two areas that need to be discussed in order to set the stage and familiarize readers with the meaning and significance of the data to follow. Chapter one presents a historical view of religious orders of women in the Catholic Church, with emphasis upon the changes that occurred during the 1960's. Religious orders as they existed in 1960, prior to the Vatican Council on Renewal, will be juxtaposed with orders as they looked ten years later, after changes had been introduced. Knowing these historical factors and having a "feel" for the dramatic and far-reaching changes that occurred in religious orders are essential in understanding the significance of the changes. Chapter two presents sociological reflections on some of the historical developments in religious orders. The latter part of the chapter presents the hypotheses that arose out of the sociological speculations and served as the "hunches" or predictions that were tested with the empirical data. A short methodological description concludes the chapter.

The three chapters that follow present and discuss the findings. Chapter three focuses upon the numbers entering and leaving religious orders during the sixties and how these rates relate to the degree of change in orders. Chapter four focuses on two organizational variables that are important in the change process, namely, level of education of the members and size of order. In Chapter five data are presented from the interviews with ex-nuns and a matched sample of nuns who remained in their orders. Chapter six ties together all the data and discusses some prognoses for the future of religious orders in the United States.

1. Religious Orders: Old and New

It was September, 1952. Presidents of Catholic religious orders of women from around the world, gathered in Rome for the International Congress of Major Superiors, were assembled, waiting for an address by Pope Pius XII, official head of the Roman Catholic Church. Even though each woman there represented a different Catholic order, and despite color differences, age differences, and ethnic differences, the group in many ways was very homogeneous. Most of the women were dressed in long, flowing robes, predominately black or brown, and had their heads covered with cloth, bonnets, and veils. In whatever language she spoke, each was addressed as mother or sister and was known as a "superior general" in the Catholic Church.

Few in the audience respectfully awaiting the arrival of the pope realized the impact of what was about to happen or the long-range effects it would have on religious orders. The pope himself probably did not fully anticipate the consequences of his remarks. He began his address by emphasizing the need within the church for dedicated nuns, women of faith living lives that are exemplary of religiously motivated behavior. The pope went on to say: "In the training of your sisters for the tasks that await them, be broadminded and liberal and admit of no stinginess. Whether it be for teaching, the care of the sick, the study of art or anything else, the Sister should be able to say to herself, 'My Superior is giving me a training that will put me on an equality with my secular colleagues.' Give them also the opportunity and the means to keep their professional knowledge up-to-date. This is important for your Sisters' peace and for their work."[1]

The majority of the superiors general in the room headed orders in which nuns taught in parochial schools, staffed Catholic hospitals, provided religious education to children and adults, and worked in social service agencies of various kinds. The pope realized that many nuns were engaged in these service occupations without proper occupational qualifications. It was common practice for a religious order to assign nuns to teach immediately after they completed high school, with no college preparation whatsoever. There were also some nuns working as nurses in Catholic hospitals and others as social workers with very little professional training. Traditionally, religious orders had placed great emphasis on spiritual development and living a dedicated religious life without concomitant emphasis upon professionalization.

An impetus for the pope's remarks was the "nun shortage" being felt in some nations throughout the world. While the Catholic population was growing and the need for parochial schools was consequently accelerating, in some orders the number of recruits was not keeping pace. Simultaneously, some nuns were leaving their religious orders. While their reasons for leaving varied, there were indications that one important reason was that some nuns felt inadequately prepared for the work they were asked to do in the church.[2] As a result, they began to question the value and meaning of their celibate commitment in a religious order.

Pope Pius XII, himself an educated man and a scholar, insisted that nuns must impart up-to-date secular knowledge as well as theological and spiritual realities. In order to obtain knowledge and training in their professional fields, nuns would have to attend universities, colleges, and professional schools. Whenever possible, they should be sent to Catholic institutions, he insisted. However, if circumstances warranted, they should also be allowed to attend secular universities.

At the conclusion of the congress, the mothers general returned to their orders throughout the world, each of them bringing back to her sisters the admonitions and recommendations of the pope. The pope's message caught on rapidly in American orders. At the time that the American superiors general were returning to this country to disseminate the message of the pope, there was a group of nuns from various orders studying at St. Louis University. This group met frequently to discuss conditions and issues within their respective orders. Concerned about the fact that many nuns were being sent out into service jobs without adequate preparation, this group of nuns, with the support of their communities, formed themselves into a movement which they called Sister Formation, in an effort to change these conditions. They toured the United States giving workshops for nuns in which they stressed the need for better professional preparation, motivated by a sense of mission in the church. In 1954 the movement was institutionalized as the Sister Formation Conference. Its express goal was to advance the sisters' spiritual and professional training. The Sister Formation Conference helped set up colleges throughout the country where sisters could receive education in secular subjects along with grounding in sound Catholic theology.[3]

The movement also emphasized the need for master's degrees and doctorates for sisters. As a result of the movement, during the 1950's and 1960's many religious orders began sending their nuns to both Catholic and secular universities for higher degrees in all areas. By the end of the 1950's and during the early 1960's, the educational levels in many communities rose significantly.

The paradox, however, was that rates of leaving religious orders increased along with educational level. Becoming better qualified professionally did not discourage nuns from opting to leave. Rather, as educational levels rose among religious orders, so did rates of exodus. This fact constitutes one of the central organizational dilemmas that religious orders have had to face during the sixties and seventies.

A hypothesis of the present study is that rates of leaving increased with education because of numerous sociological factors associated with conditions of acquiring better professional education. Most orders did not have their own colleges and universities. Therefore, many attended secular colleges and lay Catholic institutions as well as the few Sister Formation colleges set up primarily for nuns. As a consequence, there was increased social contact with both men and women outside the cloister. No longer did nuns associate only with other nuns; they began to mingle on a daily basis with single and married people, some of whom had no religious commitment whatsoever. Nuns were exposed to life-styles that provided alternatives to a celibate and highly committed religious life. While many returned to their orders with renewed commitment, others decided to leave their orders and take up, once again, a lay life outside the cloister.

In addition to increased social contacts, nuns were also exposed to new intellectual approaches. In the former system, nuns were sheltered from all worldly events by restrictions on visitors, newspapers, radios, and books. Suddenly, nuns were in the midst of the world, especially an academic world dedicated to questioning. Customs and norms previously accepted and reinforced by isolation from any groups that differed from them were put into bold focus by comparison with the broader society, which often questioned or rejected these customs and norms. For the first time in the history of orders, nuns were also exposed to a variety of intellectual positions, not only in contemporary theology but in secular subjects as well. The former dictum that dominated religious orders, that of accepting the word of the superior in "blind obedience," was replaced by the academic dictum of questioning and criticizing notions of reality and truth. The Sister Formation Movement had unanticipated consequences for religious orders, consequences that were so great and touched such vital areas of religious orders that history might well show that the Sister Formation Movement marked the beginning of the fragmentation of religious orders in the United States.

The organizational dilemma religious orders faced stemmed from the fact that pressures were being brought to bear upon them for increased educational preparation on the part of nuns. Not only was the pope himself encouraging better educational and professional backgrounds for nuns, but also the educational boom in parochial school enrollments during the 1950's meant that more and more parents were demanding quality education for their children. In 1950, the number of Catholic schools in the United States was 10,884 compared with 9,629 in 1945. By 1960, that number had risen to 12,805. Nineteen sixty-five was the peak year for Catholic schools, with 13,396 in the United States. As Catholic schools increased in number, so did the numbers of nuns teaching in them. In 1945 there were 77,847 nuns teaching in Catholic schools compared with 104,314 in 1965.[4] The increase in the number of Catholic schools during the 1950's stemmed in part from the population boom of the post–World War II years. These children were reaching school age in the decade of the fifties. Not only were Catholic parents sending their children to parochial schools, but increasing numbers of non-Catholics were choosing Catholic schools for their children because they felt these schools were providing quality education.

In addition to the pressures nuns felt from greater demands for quality education in the increasing numbers of Catholic schools, nuns themselves were beginning to realize that they were living in a society in which a knowledge explosion was occurring. To prepare children adequately for such a society, they would have to keep abreast of trends and developments. Then, too, religious leaders and theologians, such as Pope Pius XII, Karl Rahner, Edward Schillebeeckx, and Pierre Teilhard de Chardin, were demonstrating that intellectualism and scholarship need not be threats to faith and religious living but are, in fact, ways of discovering God's presence in the world and making others aware of it. Becoming well-qualified professionals, these theologians insisted, was essential to living out religious commitment within service-oriented orders.

At the same time, however, in the very process of acquiring the knowledge and skills necessary for becoming better qualified professionally, nuns came into contact with ideas and life-styles that, for many of them, threatened their commitment within the order. The result was that the women who remained in their orders were actually better prepared for their work. However, the number of such committed nuns dwindled as many opted not to remain.

Vatican Council II

By the end of the 1950's, many nuns throughout the United States were questioning the relevance to contemporary conditions of the constitutions and customs of their orders. For example, some began to wonder why nuns must wear distinctive garb, what function such clothing played in the role of nuns in the Catholic Church and in the world. Other nuns, aware of the importance of mass communication in modern society, initiated discussions of why nuns were forbidden to read newspapers or watch television. On a deeper level, many educated nuns who had been trained in philosophy and church history began to ask such questions as: What is the role of nuns in the modern world? Is this service meaningful and relevant? What is the value of a celibate religious life? Does it free a woman for more conscious and committed service in the church? What is the future of religious orders? In what ways must they adapt to the changing world? These questions created an intellectual environment that was becoming more and more common among nuns.

This was the context in which American religious orders found themselves at the time that Pope John XXIII convened the Second Vatican Council in 1962. The council fathers had determined in the early days of the council that one of the items on the agenda was a discussion of religious orders in the contemporary world. Nuns, therefore, were forewarned that a rethinking of life within religious orders was to take place during the council.

On October 28, 1965, Vatican Council II promulgated a document entitled "Decree on the Appropriate Renewal of the Religious Life."[5] The decree is summarized in one of its opening paragraphs: "The appropriate renewal of religious life involves two simultaneous processes: (1) a continuous return to the sources of all Christian life and to the original inspiration behind a given community, and (2) an adjustment of the community to the changed conditions of the time." Every religious order was encouraged to analyze its goals and structures in the light of these two guiding principles and to effect necessary changes.

In October, 1966, Pope Paul VI issued the letter *Motu Proprio* to the superiors general of all religious orders, stipulating specific means of implementing the previous council decree. In particular, every major superior was mandated to convoke within three years a special "renewal chapter," a council of elected delegates who would study the life-style and structure of their order to determine how the order could most effectively renew itself in the light of the decree. *Motu Proprio* encouraged each order to initiate experimentation with diverse forms of life-style and permitted formally approved constitutions of the order to be replaced by interim bylaws. Change, therefore, was not only allowed but mandated by the pope himself.

The nuns who read and responded to the council document on renewal and the letter of implementation were a post–Sister Formation audience. This fact no doubt affected the kind of response American nuns gave to the recommendations of the pope and bishops. One of the key instructions in the decree was that every nun should take part in examining and reorganizing religious life according to the principles set forth in the decree. By the time the decree was issued, many orders had in their membership women with advanced degrees and training in various disciplines. Therefore, not only theological expertise was brought to bear in the implementation of the council decree but also insights from history, sociology, psychology, and almost every other discipline imaginable.

"Decree on the Appropriate Renewal of the Religious Life," issued by the council fathers, and Pope Paul's letter of implementation introduced changes into religious orders that affected the very foundations of the institution. Religious life after Vatican II looked very different from religious life previous to the council. Since the nature, process, and consequences of these changes in religious orders constitute a major focus of the present book, this chapter presents a detailed picture of American religious orders in 1960, prior to the council decree. Then will follow a description of a more or less typical religious order as it looked in 1970. The consideration of orders at two time periods will highlight the extent of the changes that occurred during the 1960's.

Overview of the History of Religious Orders of Women

We began this chapter with Pope Pius XII's words to superiors general in 1952. The question remains, what was happening in religious orders in the previous two thousand years? Where did they start? Where did their roots lie? What precedents for religious orders are hidden in the primitive and medieval church?

Religious orders, in their basic elements, are as old as the Catholic Church itself. In fact, just as Christianity is foreshadowed in Old Testament Judaism, the functions of religious orders were carried out in the pre-Christian, Jewish community by women who dedicated their lives to serving special needs of the Jewish people.[6] It is in the New Testament, however, that the roots of religious orders are really established. Jesus lived a life of poverty, celibacy, and obedience. In imitation of him and in order to witness his message to the world, numerous Christian communities arose in the first century A.D. Members of these communities lived together and shared property in common. Celibacy was advocated as a primary Christian value for members who felt called to that way of life, and converts were instructed in the religious significance of a celibate life given entirely to God.

In the writings of St. Paul (1 Timothy 5:3–17) explicit mention is made of virgins and widows, women who had committed themselves to a celibate way of life after their husbands died. These virgins and widows vowed consecrated celibacy "for the sake of the kingdom" and were given special rank in the early church. A custom grew up in many places of giving those committed to celibacy a special place in Christian gatherings for public worship although they did not yet live in groups but in a secluded way in their own families. By the second century, virgins and widows were clearly distinguished, the former living a secluded life devoted chiefly to prayer and meditation and the latter engaged in an active mission in the church.

During the second and third centuries, when the early church was suffering persecutions, virginity and asceticism came to be looked upon not as ends in themselves but as preparations for martyrdom. In the fourth century, with the cessation of the persecutions, the goal of martyrdom was replaced by that of a life deliberately planned as a separation from concerns of the world and a concentration on spiritual matters. By the fourth century, celibate religious women dedicated to the glory of God were given a public ceremony of consecration and were placed under the official direction of the bishop.[7]

The first organized form of religious life was begun by St. Anthony of Egypt, who gathered a group of male disciples around him. While each person lived in a separate cell, the group would meet occasionally for common worship. At about the same time, St. Pachomius initiated a communal life for individuals who desired to give their entire selves to God. The group lived in monastic compounds with large numbers of people similarly dedicated. St. Pachomius also composed the first set of guidelines or constitutions of which there is evidence. Mary, the sister of Pachomius, headed a monastery of some four hundred women near Pachomius' monastery for men at Tabennisi. Under the direction of St. Jerome, the Roman woman Paula and her daughter Eustochium also founded three convents near Bethlehem, under the rule of Pachomius.[8]

Toward the end of the fourth century, the first convents for women spread to the great cities of the West. St. Ambrose and St. Augustine paid great attention to them. A letter from St. Augustine to one of these convents was later developed into the Rule of St. Augustine, which many contemporary convents still follow. The rule stresses the value of common life and the need for abstinence and authority for people living together for religious purposes.

St. Benedict of Nursia, in the sixth century, introduced a way of life that was to become part of the Western church until contemporary times. In his conception, religious life centered on the abbot, the spiritual father of the monastery and administrator of all the temporalities of the community. The monastery was to form a society independent from the outside world, self-contained and characterized by charity and dedication to prayer. While St. Benedict himself did not envision a religious life for women, his rule was applied to women in England, and from the middle of the eighth century until the twelfth century it was the most common rule for women.

The medieval church saw the development of the mendicant orders whose members did not belong to one house but to an entire order. Each order was divided into provinces under the administration of a single superior. Members owned no material goods and received their financial support from begging or from their own work. The two largest mendicant orders were the Franciscans, founded by St. Francis of Assisi, and the Dominicans, founded by St. Dominic. Both groups established orders for women that followed the same general rules and customs as their male counterparts.

The twelfth and thirteenth centuries were the times of the great barbarian invasions. It was common for the barbarian intruders to rape women in the countries they were conquering, and celibate nuns were not excluded. As a protection against the invaders, Pope Boniface VIII in 1283, in the decree *Periculosa*, established the idea of the cloister for Catholic nuns to separate them physically from the rest of the world. It was in this period that huge convent walls and moats around convent buildings became common.[9] After the threat of the invasion was over, the notion of the cloister extended beyond just physical isolation. It took on great symbolic and religious significance as well as psychological meaning. Nuns were isolated within the cloister not just for protection against physical harm, but, in a deeper sense, for protection against worldliness and the lures of society.

Until the sixteenth century, the members of all religious orders took solemn vows, that is, public vows taken for life, which included the renunciation of all ownership of material goods, the renunciation of marriage and family, and the renunciation of acting totally in accord with one's own desires. Solemn vows were lived out in a cloistered context in which members were totally secluded from the larger society. The cloister became a mechanism and a means for assisting nuns in the living out of their vows. In the sixteenth century, the Jesuits were founded, a society of men who vowed to go anywhere in the world the pope might send them for the needs of the church. They introduced the practice of "simple vows," vows of poverty, chastity, and obedience, practiced outside of strict contemplative, totally isolated enclosures.[10]

In 1533, Angela Merici founded the Ursuline Sisters and gave them a task and life-style unheard of before that time. The Ursuline order was founded to teach young girls. In order to do this, the nuns wore no fixed garb, shared no community life, and lived within no customary enclosure. Rather, these religious women lived alone or in small groups and were totally dedicated to their teaching mission. Angela Merici never gained ecclesiastical approbation for her order but recruits continued to join.

The institution of the Daughters of Charity by St. Vincent de Paul in the early eighteenth century marked a new beginning for religious women in the church. Because this service-oriented group was officially recognized as an ecclesiastical order, the enclosure with its emphasis on concentration and removal from the world was replaced by orders dedicated to the goal of apostolic service. The Daughters of Charity had as their primary emphasis caring for the health needs of people. Numerous other orders were subsequently founded to teach, do missionary work, care for orphans, and serve many other needs in the church. While members in these congregations lived together and shared a common prayer life, their primary work was caring for the needs of people. Celibacy remained instrumental in that it freed the religiously dedicated woman for complete service to the church.

During the 1700's small groups of religious women came from Europe to the New World to serve specific needs of immigrant groups. However, religious orders in America can be dated from July, 1809, when Elizabeth Seton founded the Sisters of Charity, dedicated to hospital work. During the Civil War, the Sisters of Charity as well as other groups that had been established in the interim gained notice and appreciation for their nursing of the wounded and prisoners. The sisters risked their own lives in calamities like the smallpox epidemic that broke out in San Francisco in March, 1868, and raged for over a year.

Just as the Catholic Church itself is an immigrant church, so are religious orders in the United States immigrant institutions.[11] The majority of orders in the United States date back to the eighteenth and nineteenth centuries, when the first nuns came to this country from the convents of Europe. The first wave of Catholic immigrants in the mid-nineteenth century came from southwest Germany. American bishops traveled to the convents of Germany to request sisters to accompany the immigrants to America to teach and nurse. The second wave of Catholic immigrants, later in the nineteenth century, came mostly from Ireland. Irish nuns settled with the immigrants in Irish communities, particularly along the eastern seaboard. In the early decades of the twentieth century, when the Poles and Italians came to this country, it became especially important for nuns to establish parochial schools in these immigrant settlements because language was a barrier to integration into American society.

The period during and after World War I was an expansionist one for the Catholic Church in America. The "triumphalist phase," as John Cogley calls it, was demonstrated in the numerous parish churches and parochial schools established throughout the country.[12] Religious orders of women grew rapidly in the post–World War I years both as a result of continued European recruiting and the recruitment of growing numbers of American girls from schools staffed by religious orders. This expansionist trend continued during the 1940's and increased in the 1950's under the impact of the Sister Formation Movement.

Entering a religious order had many implications for Catholic girls, particularly those of immigrant parents. In addition to the recognition and prestige that accrued to parents whose daughters were Catholic nuns, joining a religious order meant an opportunity to gain an education and to have a meaningful career, an opportunity which frequently was not available to Catholic girls of first- or second-generation immigrant parents. In addition, most of the girls entering religious orders were products of Catholic parochial schools, where nuns were held before them as models of a meaningful, good life. Becoming a nun, therefore, was a highly acceptable and rewarded option for girls who had completed grammar school, especially for girls who were not particularly attracted to the usual role of wife and mother.

The Sister Formation Movement in the fifties had set up numerous "aspirancies," where girls were accepted at the beginning of their high school years and trained during high school in the principles of religious life as well as in secular high school subjects. Therefore, during the 1950's many orders had large numbers of girls preparing to become nuns.

Pre–Vatican II Religious Orders

Prior to the Sister Formation Movement and Vatican Council II, religious orders in the United States were quite homogeneous both in exterior manifestations and in the purpose and spirit that permeated them. The fact that orders responded to the call for renewal and change at different paces meant that during the latter half of the 1960's the homogeneity among orders decreased. However, because similar changes were introduced into the various orders during the renewal process, today religious orders are again looking more and more alike, although very different from the way they looked a decade ago. The following description of pre–Vatican II orders is typical of most orders during this period.

Unifying Myths

A central characteristic of pre–Vatican II religious orders was the social and psychological totalism of thought, attitudes, and behavior demanded of members. The goal, as stated formally in most constitutions, was to dedicate one's life totally to glorifying God and serving his church. Every rule and regulation in the order was established to achieve this goal.

One of the most insightful analyses of psychological totalism is found in Robert Lifton's *Thought Reform and the Psychology of Totalism.*[13] Lifton bases his analysis on a study of brainwashing among the Chinese prisoners. While the Chinese Communists were trying to inculcate goals and attitudes different from those in religious orders, the process of creating a totalistic environment is very similar. In the description of pre–Vatican II orders that follows, many of Lifton's ideas are utilized to understand what was occurring. By demonstrating the similarity of the thought reform processes in two divergent settings, I hope the impact of Lifton's analysis will be strengthened.

Lifton maintains that the purpose of all totalistic thought reform is to achieve "ideological totalism," that is, "any set of emotionally charged convictions about man and his relation to the natural or supernatural world."[14] While any ideology may be carried by its adherents in a totalistic direction, ideological totalism is most likely to occur with those ideologies which are most sweeping in their content or most messianic, whether religious, political, or scientific. The basic element in ideological totalism is its all-or-nothing character, that is, the harnessing of all energies and attention for the attainment of a single world view.

Central to ideological totalism is the construction of a thought system that is utilized to interpret and give meaning to all reality. George Sorel defines such a comprehensive thought system as a myth, that is, a world view that attempts to explain why certain phenomena were, are, or shall be. The relative truth or untruth of a myth is unimportant. Members do not *understand* a myth—they feel, experience, and believe in it as the ultimate explanation for what is.[15] Members are less interested in proving the reality of the myth than in living it out in daily life. What sustains the unifying myth is consensual validation by the group.[16] The myth is supported by the fact that others also believe it and are willing to live out their lives in terms of it.

Membership in every religious order demanded radical commitment whereby the individual member gave up many of the normal rewards and pleasures enjoyed in day-to-day life outside the cloister, such as sexual enjoyment; family life; property and material possessions; a large measure of independence over one's life; and deciding how to spend one's day, what leisure activities to enjoy, and what friends to have. What made such radical denial possible and meaningful was the theological and ideological system of thought and values that supported the relationship between personal sacrifice and higher goals. There existed a unifying central myth which was powerful enough to call forth total commitment of group members.

Religious orders in the Catholic Church shared a general myth as well as myths unique to each particular order. In general, religious orders viewed their purpose as total dedication to living a Christian life and thereby giving example to others of a perfect way of life. Members did this by going into a cloister, in order to be able to concentrate solely upon living the life Jesus preached for all Christians. Every structure, norm, and institutionalized behavior pattern in religious orders was set up explicitly and publicly for living a Christian life. Basic Christian theology, therefore, became the central myth around which life as a nun was organized. That central myth might be summarized as follows:

> God, as Father, created the world and made man to share in His Divine Life. Through sin and pride man disobeyed and offended God and therefore man was no longer worthy to share in God's life. Christ was sent by the loving Father to redeem man and restore him to grace, that is, to life with God. The Catholic Church was established by Christ as a means to grace and to eternal salvation. Grace is the participation of man in God's supernatural life. Only to the extent that selfishness and pride are eradicated can

God's grace operate effectively in the soul, to make man godlike. According to the example given by the God-man, Christ, the whole of the Christian life is to "put on Christ," as St. Paul preached, or to be Christlike, so that God's grace can engulf and direct a Christian's total life. In order to "put on Christ" it is necessary for the Christian to empty himself of all natural impulses and what is not of God so that he can be totally filled by God. (Paraphrased summary of descriptions from Dom Marmion's *Christ, the Life of the Soul*)

Christian redemption as seen by the nun was not an act completed two thousand years ago on a hill in Galilee but was rather a continuous process accomplished by the death of the individual to all worldly attitudes, motivations, and actions and rebirth to a life imbued with supernatural, otherworldly motivations. The two-pronged process of death to oneself and rebirth to God summarized the meaning behind all of the highly routinized and institutionalized modes of behavior characteristic of the fifteen centuries of religious orders.

Lifton describes this basic process of death and rebirth as characteristic of any type of radical thought reform and resocialization of behavior. To achieve ideological totalism or to bring persons into a completely new world view to which they are completely committed, whether in religion, political movements, or scientific organizations, always demands some type of death and rebirth process. In religious orders, the twofold process of death and rebirth was shaped by the central Christian myth and kept alive by daily reading and exhortations.

1. *Death unto oneself.* Many of the customs and structures of religious life were set up to accomplish the negation and denial of natural desires and impulses. In her early training, every nun was frequently exposed to "spiritual reading books," books whose central message was death to self. Dom Columba Marmion's *Christ, the Life of the Soul*, for example, exhorts nuns as follows:

If we wish nothing to interpose between us and God, nothing to hinder our union with Him, if we wish divine blessings to flow in upon our souls, we must not only renounce sin and imperfection, but moreover strip ourselves of our personality, in so far as it constitutes an obstacle to perfect union with God. It constitutes an obstacle to perfect union when our judgment, our self will, our self love, our susceptibilities make us think and act otherwise than according to the desires of our Heavenly Father. . . . when the soul arrives at a state of having stripped itself of all sin and all attachments to self and creatures, of having destroyed in itself as far as possible all purely natural and human springs of action in order to surrender itself completely to the Divine action, of living an absolute dependence on God, on His will, His commandments, in the spirit of the gospel, of conferring everything to the Heavenly Father, then we can truly say "The Lord ruleth me, everything in me comes from Him, I am in His hands." This soul has attained to the perfect imitation of Christ, to the point where his life is the very reproduction of that of Christ.[17]

Another book that shaped the thinking and attitudes of nuns was *The Imitation of Christ*, a series of imaginary dialogues between Christ and the person seeking perfection. Excerpts were read aloud at breakfast each morning, and many orders required nuns to memorize passages from it. The eighth chapter of book three is typical of the book. The passage presents the person speaking to Christ:

Shall I, Lord Jesus, that am but dust and ashes, dare speak to thee? Verily do I think myself any better than ashes and dust; thou standest against me and my own sins also bear witness against me. If I despise myself and set myself as naught, and think myself but ashes and dust as I am, then thy grace should be light unto me and the light of pure understanding shall enter into my heart, so that all presumption and pride in me shall be drowned in the veil of meekness through perfect humility of my wretchedness.[18]

As these two excerpts demonstrate, the death-to-self process consisted not only of external, peripheral behavioral measures but also a total reorientation and reorganization of the person's deepest attitudes and motivations, a complete and radical restructuring of basic thought patterns, self-perceptions, and attitudes. It was, in Lifton's phrase, "ideological totalism," in which the totality of one's personality was eradicated and then radically restructured. Again from the *Imitation of Christ*, the following paragraph demonstrates the depth of the theological reorientation demanded of the nun trying to live out this central, unifying Christian myth. This time Christ is speaking:

Always and in every hour, in great things and in small, mayest thou be mine and I thine unless thou be clearly bereft of thy own will within and without. The sooner thou canst bring it about, so much the sooner shall it be better with thee and the more perfectly and more closely thou canst do it the more shalt thou please me, the more shalt thou win. Some persons resign themselves unto me but it is with some exceptions for they trust not fully to me and therefore they study to provide for themselves. Surely these persons shall never come to perfect cleanness and freedom of heart nor to the grace of familiarity with me but through a perfect forsaking of themselves and all that they have wholly to me for without this no man can unite perfectly with me.[19]

Through constant study and reading of these passages, nuns became imbued with the necessity of dying to self. In addition, they were required to confess during public ceremonies acts of selfishness and pride which were transgressions against the central purpose of religious life.

2. *Rebirth to a life of union with God*. The purpose of the death-to-self process was to empty the soul of selfishness so that God could fill the soul. The natural and the supernatural were seen as two dichotomous poles within individuals. Only to the extent that a person could control and regulate her human feelings and desires could she be open to the supernatural movements of the spirit. Marmion's book describes how the process of rebirth takes place through an imitation of Jesus Christ:

Christ indeed is not only a model, such as the artist contemplates when he paints a portrait. Neither can we compare the imitation of Jesus Christ to the superficial imitation obtained by some when they copy the actions and gestures of a great man they admire, an imitation that does not reach the soul. Christ is more than a model, more than a High Priest, who has obtained for us the grace to imitate Him. He himself by His Spirit acts in the sanctuary of the soul, acts to help us imitate Him. Why is that? Because as I said in speaking of the Divine Plan, our holiness is of an essentially supernatural order. God is not content and never will be content since He has resolved on making us His children. He wills us to act as children of Divine grace.[20]

The purpose of religious life, therefore, was to assist members to live a supernaturally oriented life by negating and rising above a purely natural mode of existence.

In many aspects, the central myth of religious life resembles the classic theme of war between good and evil. In *Paradise Lost* Milton describes the struggle in dramatic terms. Faust's dialogue with the devil projects the warring impulses between good and evil. The unifying myth in many utopian communities evolves from this cosmic struggle. The Bruderhof, for example, see the universe as involved in a death struggle between good and evil. God is at the head of the forces of good, which will ultimately triumph. Man can help by emptying himself of ego and allowing himself to be filled with the Holy Spirit.[21] The good-and-evil myth in religious life, therefore, takes on its unique meanings to the extent that it is given Christian content. Good is defined in relation to an anthropomorphic Father and a personal Savior. Evil is personified in a devil and as the consequence of original sin. Man overcomes evil and embodies good by denying his natural tendencies toward pride and selfishness and being filled with divine, supernatural life.

In addition to the general Christian myth, which is the encompassing purpose of all religious orders, each order lived out this myth in somewhat different ways, depending on the purposes and spirit of its founder. Specific virtues and religious practices were emphasized by the founder. These specific religious qualities made belonging to a given order distinct from membership in any other order.

It is crucial for an understanding of religious orders to penetrate deeply into the meanings these unifying myths had for the members in order to understand how they could make the sacrifices, self-denials, and commitment required for membership. External structures and daily activities cannot be understood without realizing the interior commitment that members made to this way of understanding and defining the world. Belonging to a religious institute was more than just following external forms or prescriptions. The primary purpose of a religious order was to penetrate the depths of a person's conception of reality so that everything was reinterpreted in the light of the myths provided to the members. The total world view became the goal and motivating force of members. In this sense, a religious order was an ideological community committed to a set of assumptions and attitudes that permeate thought and behavior on a day-by-day basis. The primary factor in sustaining these myths and reinforcing them constantly was that members lived as an in-group isolated from persons who thought otherwise. The myth, therefore, became reality, and, in Peter Berger's terms, the group became a community of believers where myths were constantly validated.[22] In order for this type of community to sustain itself, it was essential that some degree of isolation from mainstream society be maintained. This was the purpose of the cloister, both in its physical and psychological aspects.

Social Control

As in all groups social control was exercised in the order in two ways: formally, through the official authority structure, and informally, through a network of customs and expectations. The basic legitimation of the formal authority structure was the central myth that God's providence and will were made known through superiors. Superiors were more than human authority figures; they were instruments of God, making his will known to members in the order. Disobedience was more than simple human disobedience; it was an act of pride against God.

According to canon law, the highest governing body of a religious order is the "general chapter," a group of representatives elected by the members. The chapter meets periodically to formulate general policies and elect a central administration, that is, the mother general and her council. Since the constitution of an order remained relatively unchanged in the traditional system, the primary task of the chapter was to elect the mother general, who then exercised considerable power in the administration of the order. She had the power to assign sisters to the jobs they were to perform, to decide where and with whom they were to live, what daily schedule they were to follow, and who was to be the local superior in each house in which sisters resided. In turn, the mother general was to receive the utmost respect of the sisters, and her voice was to be recognized as manifesting the "will of God" to the sisters.

The superior general, according to the constitution of the order, was to govern and administer the entire congregation according to the constitution. She had the right of entrusting offices and employments which pertained to the congregation and hence the right of assigning sisters to houses and provinces. It was her duty to see that all the sisters, "superiors as well as inferiors," made use of the same dress and furnishings.

The local superiors, to whom were committed the administration of their respective houses, were bound to ensure the observance of the constitution and to preside at all community exercises. The various duties and employments in the house, such as sacristan of the chapel, purchaser of food and household goods, and financial treasurer of the house, were usually assigned to the sisters by the local superiors, frequently in consultation with their counselors. The local superiors could grant leave to any sister to travel, but in many orders only if the sister could return home the same day. They could also give permission for the sisters to make use of personal gifts provided that the value of these material goods did not exceed the stipulated amount. The local superiors were to give instruction on Christian doctrine, adapted to the capacity of the hearers, and a pious exhortation to all the members of the house.

The sisters, on the other hand, were instructed by the constitution to obey their superiors and be submissive to them in small matters as well as large ones. At the superior's voice, all were instructed to be most ready to obey instantly, leaving any occupation whatever. Since it was impossible for the superior herself to see and hear all things, the sisters were commanded to be willing to manifest to the superior all personal errors, defects, and temptations, and to be willing to be corrected.

"Order of precedence" was carefully described in the constitution, by which the superior general held first place in the congregation. After her came her counselors, the secretary general and treasurer general, then the other sisters according to the times of their first profession of vows. Normally, sisters entered the dining room and chapel according to their rank and sat accordingly.

The system of social control in pre–Vatican II religious orders closely followed the model described by Lifton in his analysis of thought reform within ideological totalism. Lifton describes eight mechanisms which he says make totalism work. Each mechanism depends upon an equally absolute philosophical assumption, and each mobilizes certain emotional tendencies, mainly of a polarizing nature.

The first mechanism of social control is what Lifton calls "milieu control." He says the most important psychological feature of the thought reform environment, upon which all else depends, is the control of human communication. Through milieu control the totalist environment seeks to establish the domain not only of an individual's communication from the outside, that is, all she or he sees and hears, but also the person's inner life, what can be called communication with oneself. Many things happen psychologically to one exposed to milieu control. Most basic is the disruption of relations between the self and the outside world. The person is deprived of the combination of external information and inner reflection required to test the realities of the environment and to maintain a measure of identity separate from it. Instead, the individual is called upon to make an absolute polarization of the real, to dichotomize the world into the prevailing ideology and everything else. To the extent that the individual does this, she undergoes what Lifton calls a "personal closure." This frees her from the struggle with subtleties of truth. Because milieu control was so prevalent in pre–Vatican II religious orders and changed dramatically in the process of renewal, this first mechanism of thought reform will be emphasized in the description of religious orders.

Milieu control was accomplished through the process of socialization whereby recruits became full-fledged nuns in the order. Socialization refers to the process whereby an individual internalizes goals, values, attitudes, and behavior patterns of a given group. While the recruit comes into the group with a self-conception, upon her entrance into a total institution it is imperative that she be stripped of the support provided by these arrangements so that a new conception of self might develop.[23]

It is essential to the process of socialization into a total institution to learn and become identified with the unifying central myth of the group. As has been described in the previous section, the individual must be stripped of certain attitudes and self-perceptions so that she may identify with the spirit and life of the group.

There were three separate stages in the socialization process: (1) the first twelve to twenty-four months in the order, known as the *postulancy*; (2) the *novitiate*, a completely cloistered year, required by canon law of the church before a woman was allowed to make vows in the order; and (3) *professed religious life*, that is, actually living with vows in the order. For the first three to six years, depending on the order, the religious made only annual vows, that is, vows that had to be renewed every year. After that initial period, they were allowed to make perpetual vows, that is, vows for life.

Each of the stages was characterized by the twofold process of self-denial and internalization of new norms and roles. At each stage the woman renounced more of herself and became more and more identified with the spirit and expectations of the order. This was achieved by controlling the convent milieu in which the individual was socialized.

The first stage of socialization typically began when a young woman presented herself in the convent parlor and asked to see the director of postulants. Entrance requirements differed during various periods in orders. At one time it was possible in many orders for a young woman to enter any time after completing grade school. It was common, therefore, to have a wide range in ages among new recruits.

Most recruits were products of schools staffed by the order. Frequently, a favorite nun became a role model for the young girl, and her dream was to become like her idol. In addition to the challenge of a life of service, the radical sacrifices asked of nuns often appealed to the idealistic spirit of youth.

After the director had welcomed the young woman and congratulated her parents for the great privilege of having a daughter chosen by God himself, the recruit was taken into the cloister to the area designated as the "postulancy." Here she exchanged her secular clothes for the black uniform of the postulant. This was the first symbolic gesture of "putting off the world" and entering into a new life. The uniform was characterized by complete simplicity and modesty, being high-necked, long-sleeved, and ankle length. In addition to the uniform, feminine lingerie was exchanged for simple white cotton underwear, indicating that the postulant was exchanging her womanly enjoyments for austere dress that would now symbolize her as the spouse of Jesus Christ. In addition, henceforth the woman was no longer to be distinguished by dress from the other women in the institute with whom she would live. This external uniformity symbolized an internal uniformity of attitudes and values which was supposed to characterize and distinguish a religious woman.

The postulant was then allowed one last good-bye to her parents in the parlor, usually with the directress of postulants present. From that moment on, all interaction with family and friends would be highly regulated. The farewell to her parents, therefore, was more than just a simple good-bye. It symbolized not only a physical separation but a pyschological one as well. Thereafter the recruit was allowed to see her family one afternoon a month in the convent parlor or on the convent grounds. After one year in the order she was allowed a week's visit at home. However, she could not sleep in the home of her family but had to visit during the day and return to a local convent for the night. Only in the event of death of a parent was she allowed to return home outside of the scheduled visits. Needless to say, weddings, celebrations, and other reunions with her family were completely forbidden. In fact, the young woman gave up her place in the family in order to become a member of a new religious family.

The postulant was asked not to bring with her any personal possessions since everything she needed would be provided by the community. There was a common closet where personal articles such as toothpaste, soap, and medicines were kept. However, the postulant had to have the permission of the superior before taking anything from the closet, no matter what the article might be. This practice prepared the young recruit for the vows of poverty and obedience she would be taking some day and for the style of life demanded of every member in the order.

Every six months or so each member itemized her clothing needs. The list had to be approved by the superior before each item was purchased or sewn by members assigned to that duty.

The postulant was allowed no money of her own, since personal funds involved individual choice and a sense of self-reliance. From entry to death the person might not experience exchange of money for goods. In effect she was exchanging her entire self and services in return for having all her needs provided by the order.

Meals in the convent were simple but plentiful. Each member was expected to take something from every dish and was not allowed to specify likes and dislikes. Instead she was taught to accept gratefully whatever was provided by the cook that day. Meals were eaten in silence except for reading from the Scriptures or some spiritual book.

Learning appropriate gestures and mannerisms was another part of the socialization process. There was a proper way to be seated at table, to eat soup, to break bread. Making noise in the dining room or while walking in the halls was completely forbidden because it disrupts recollection and union with God. There was also a proper way to walk. One postulant, for example, was required to spend afternoon after afternoon following her superior down the hall in order to get rid of her "worldly walk." She was told that she held her head too high, moved her hips too much, and bounced in a very worldly fashion and that if she expected to enter the order as a professed member she would have to learn a "religious walk." Extreme movements of the body were defined as distractions and obstacles to a recollected spirit. There was a proper way to hold one's skirt going up and down stairs, a proper way to rise when a superior entered the room, a proper way to address superiors, to square dance, to play baseball. All slang and profane language was forbidden. Nicknames were considered improper. Constant recollection and prayer demanded modesty or "custody" of the eyes, that is, keeping one's eyes downcast regardless of what was going on. For example, if a stranger entered the dining room, it was inappropriate to raise one's eyes. The body was considered a gift of God, sacred; it was not created for enjoyment or distraction but as an instrument to do God's will.

Most of the candidates attended classes during the academic year. Studying was taken very seriously because it was seen as preparation for doing God's work. Secular girls frequently attended the high school and college where candidates studied; however, there was no interaction between the two groups. The candidates were to walk to class together as a group and were not to greet or talk to anyone en route. In the classroom, the candidates sat together and were not to interact with seculars. After class, the group of candidates were to return to the convent together without lingering in the classrooms or in the halls.

The purpose of all rituals and regulations was to develop in the recruit a sense of her new life and the importance of utilizing every moment and opportunity to further her union with God. She was instructed daily in ways of prayer and virtuous living and how to achieve constant awareness of the presence of God. In order to accomplish this state of constant prayer, self-discipline and meditation were essential.

The young woman had frequent consultations with a spiritual director, either a priest or a superior, who assisted her in her ascent to spiritual heights.

If the candidate persisted and demonstrated that she was capable of living a religious life, after twelve to twenty-four months of formal training she was accepted as a novice into the order. The year of the novitiate was completely cloistered; the individual had no contact with members outside the novitiate group. In fact, she was even isolated from professed members of the order, so that her entire concentration for 365 days was on the Lord alone and what a life totally dedicated to him under vows would mean.

The ceremony during which postulants became novices was a highly symbolic rite of passage. In the minds of parents and friends outside the cloister, this ceremony represented the moment when they visualized the young woman becoming a nun. The ceremony was preceded by a ten-day contemplative retreat during which the young woman prepared herself for total dedication of her life to God. With family and friends gathered in the chapel for the rite, the group of postulants proceeded into the chapel dressed in white bridal gowns and veils, to symbolize their becoming brides of Jesus Christ. Before the bishop, the group sang a traditional hymn, which was a bridal chant, during which they bowed in humility and submission to their bridegroom, Christ. They were then formally given the habit of a nun by the bishop, after which they retired to the sacristy of the church to exchange their bridal attire for the religious garb. Part of the transformation process included cutting the woman's hair very short so that it would fit under the coif and bonnet of the nun. This was done by nonhairdressers, with no thought of style or shape. Frequently members commented on the trauma involved in having their hair cut in this fashion. The symbolism of giving up what has often been considered woman's glory is that the nun is publicly renouncing worldliness and donning an otherworldly religious spirit.

After returning to the chapel, the newly habited nun received a religious name from the bishop, a name of some saint in the church, symbolizing her new identity. This name, chosen for her by the superior general, was prefaced by the title "Sister." The fact that frequently the person received a male name indicated that sexual differences were no longer emphasized.

The third stage in the socialization process was religious profession. After one year as a novice, the nun formally requested entrance into the order as a professed member. Her request was considered by the superior general and her council, who then voted on whether they deemed her suitable as a member of the order. If allowed to stay, the nun took annual vows for a specified number of years, usually three to six years. If at the end of that period she desired to make a life commitment and the order decided to accept her as a permanent member, she made final or perpetual vows for life. In order to be released from perpetual vows, permission was required from Rome, so serious did the church consider the step. Dispensation from final vows was given only for serious reasons, such as the desire to marry.

The vows a religious woman took were threefold: poverty, chastity, and obedience. By the vow of poverty, the nun gave up the use of material goods and property of her own. On a day-to-day, practical level, this meant that the nun relied completely upon the order for subsistence. In a more minute sense, it meant she had to have permission of the superior for the use of any goods whatsoever. Permissions were an integral part of the daily life in the order. They were required for the use of all personal articles, foods, doctor visits, telephone calls, textbooks, writing materials—in short, the use of any material goods. The purpose behind the permission system was to remind the nun that she was poor and owned nothing. Positively, it reminded her of complete dependence upon God.

By chastity the nun gave up all sexual involvement and all activities having sexual connotations, such as dating. She willingly accepted a celibate way of life and renounced having a spouse and family. Positively, she accepted Jesus Christ as the motivation and goal of her life. By obedience, she promised submission to legitimate superiors, both in the larger church and in the order. The spirit behind obedience was that God's will would be made known to her through her superior.

The taking of final vows meant that the woman became a full-fledged, permanent member of the order. During her initial formation period, the young woman had little contact with anyone outside the cloister. Rather, she lived in close proximity with others who were preparing for a life of total religious dedication. Any contact with outsiders had been highly regulated. Newspapers, radios, and televisions had been forbidden or curtailed so that contact with the outside through the media had also been minimal. Such extreme cloistering provided optimal opportunity for the order to instill within the members those attitudes, values, and behaviors that constituted a nun's way of life.

Religious orders accomplished milieu control most vividly and successfully through the enforcement of the cloister. Members were removed from contact with outsiders and forced to interact solely with in-group members. In addition to proscriptions against contact with family and friends except under highly regulated conditions, all letters and correspondence coming into the cloister were opened and censored by superiors, who had freedom to withhold from members any information which they judged to be threats to the religious vocation of the members. Similarly, all letters written to nongroup members were also read. Personal contact with outsiders was highly controlled.

When it was mandatory for members to go to town to see a doctor or to make purchases for the community, they never went alone but were accompanied by another member. When outsiders came to the house to visit a sister they were always to be received in the parlor. Without permission of the superior, the sister could not meet them or hold conversation with them. No sister could spend an undue amount of time in the parlor. Whenever advisable the superior was to appoint a companion for a sister entertaining visitors. Never, even for the smallest amount of time, were members to be alone with men unless the door were open; and never, no matter what the cause, could men, even priests, remain overnight within the cloister. Although modesty was always to be evident in the sisters' demeanor, it was to be especially manifest in the presence of men. They were never to allow themselves even the slightest familiarity with men.

The cloister, therefore, is a prime example of Lifton's milieu control. Evil and danger were seen in persons and reality outside the cloister which were a threat to the inner life of members in the order, while religious values promoted by the cloister were defined as good. In a profound sense, the cloister and its concomitant structures were established to promote milieu control and thereby control of the behavior of members within the cloister.

The second mechanism Lifton describes in the process of achieving ideological totalism is "mystical manipulation," that is, the creation of a sense of higher purpose, of having inside knowledge of a higher purpose, or goal of human development.[24] Any thought or action which questions the higher purpose is considered to be stimulated by a lower purpose, to be backward, selfish, and petty in the face of the great overriding mission. At the level of the individual person, psychological responses to such a manipulative approach revolve around the basic polarity of trust and mistrust. The person is asked to accept manipulation as a basis of absolute trust "like a child in the arms of his mother." Faithful members can experience trust and find pleasure in their pain because of their endorsement of the higher purpose as their own.

In religious orders this mystical manipulation took place through the unifying central myth which defined authority as supernatural. Members were obeying not only natural authority but also the divine will of

God himself. To disobey was sinful. This mystical sense of obedience extended to the most minute details of members' lives, such as times of rising and retiring, times to pray, eat, bathe, speak, keep silent.

Lifton's third instrument of thought reform is what he calls "demand for purity." He says, "In the thought-reform milieu as in all situations of ideological totalism, the experiental world is sharply divided into the pure and the impure, into the absolutely good and the absolutely evil. The good and the pure are, of course, those ideas, feelings and actions which are consistent with the totalist ideology and policy; anything else is apt to be relegated to the bad and the impure."[25] Lifton goes on to say that by defining and manipulating the criteria of purity and then by conducting an all-out war on impurity, ideological totalists create a narrow world of guilt and shame. Each person's impurity is sinful and potentially harmful to himself and others. Moreover, the sense of guilt and shame becomes a highly valued object of communication and competition and the basis for bonds between the individual and his totalist superiors. Superiors, then, become arbiters of existential guilt. Their power is nowhere more evident than in their capacity to forgive.

Without doubt, the most profound mechanisms of social control within religious orders lie in this realm of the definition of the pure and the impure, the sacred and profane. Sociologists of religion have frequently distinguished between the sacred and the profane, the holy and the secular. All people have some notion of what is holy and unholy. However they define the holy, it constitutes a central world view. In religious orders, the notion of the sacred and the profane permeated every aspect of daily living. Basically, whatever sprang from God and religious motivations was sacred, whatever was of the world and not of God was evil.

In religious orders, the sacred extended to places, times, persons, ideas, and things. Certain rooms in the cloister were defined as sacred, for example, the chapel, dining room, and recreation room. One indication of this sacredness was the regulation that there be no talking in these rooms except with explicit permission of the superior. To speak in the dining room constituted an offense of the constitution of the order. There is no way to explain why some of these places were considered sacred. They simply became so through tradition. Similarly, certain times of the day were set aside as sacred. The explicit purpose of silence was to provide a milieu in which the person could more easily commune with God and focus thoughts on him. Silence was so pervasive in the life of the nun that, rather than specify times of silence, the constitution specified times of talking. All other times were sacred and silence was to be observed. In addition, the period from the time of retiring until the next morning after breakfast was defined in the constitution as the "sacred silence." To speak during this time was an offense against the constitution and was to be confessed during public "culpa," that is, the ritual of public confession of transgressions against the constitution.

Certain persons were considered sacred within the religious order, primarily the superior, who represented the voice of God in the community. Rituals of respect developed around the superior, such as rising when she entered a room, allowing her to precede through a doorway, and tending to her personal needs, such as making her bed, cleaning her room, and keeping her clothing mended and laundered. Things were also sacred. For example, the habit was called the "holy habit," and when donning it, the nun was obliged to cite specific prayers and to kiss each piece as it was put on. The sacredness of this habit was contained in its symbolism as the garb of a bride of Christ totally dedicated to him.

It is evident that respect for the sacred was not simply a behavioral response. It was also an attitudinal orientation. It was possible, therefore, for such conformity to be enforced externally, but the primary mechanism of control was guilt or shame.

Emile Durkheim and other anthropologists frequently discussed the concept taboo. Taboo means that there is a source of sacred things which will cause harm to those persons who do not respect and honor the sacred things. Individuals will arouse the anger of the gods if the rules of the sacred are not minutely obeyed.[26] Similarly, in religious orders not only was internal guilt utilized but the notion of God's disfavor and evil befalling the person was so rampant that to perform a tabooed activity tended to arouse tremendous guilt in the individual. Guilt was dispelled primarily through public confession. Culpa referred to the exercise in religious orders in which members of the order congregated to publicly profess their faults and failings against aspects of the constitution. It was common to hear such self-accusations as "I spoke during sacred silence," "I was late for spiritual exercises," or "I have not been kissing the holy habit." To confess these transgressions against the community and to experience forgiveness by fellow community members provided relief for shame and guilt. In addition to culpa, it was common for nuns to ask direct forgiveness from superiors for transgressions as they occurred. For example, when a sister came late for a community exercise, she was expected to approach the superior and ask forgiveness. The ritual consisted in her bowing before the superior and asking forgiveness. This ritual was an extension of confession in the Catholic Church, where the priest represents Jesus Christ and publicly forgives the sinner.

In addition to shame and guilt and the myriad of mechanisms which involved social control, there were periodic reports sent by the superior to higher superiors in regard to each individual member. For example, before the member was permitted to make her vows, a detailed report of her spiritual and psychological progress was sent to the superior general and her council. In conference, these higher superiors decided if the member was worthy to proceed in religious life. Therefore, there was constant fear that these secret reports would contain statements that would hinder the individual's remaining in the order.

Lifton describes the "cult of confession" and making faults public as the fourth mechanism of social control.[27] He says this obsession with personal confession is related to the demand for absolute purity.

The fifth state in thought reform is what Lifton calls "the sacred science."[28] The totalist milieu contains an aura of sacredness around its basic dogma, pointing it out as an ultimate moral vision for the ordering of human existence. The sacredness is evident in each of the basic assumptions. At the level of the individual, the totalist sacred science can offer much comfort and security. So strong a hold can the sacred achieve over mental processes that when one begins to feel herself attracted to ideas which either contradict or ignore it she becomes guilty and afraid. The person's submission becomes more difficult because of the absence in totalist environments of any realm untouched by holiness and its demands. There is no thought or action, therefore, which cannot be related to the sacred science. In religious orders the unifying central myth was defined as absolute truth. The myth became not one way of viewing reality but the only way. In order to maintain the myth and avoid ideas which might endanger it, reading material and exposure to alien thought were highly controlled. The myth was so encompassing that all of reality was defined in terms of it.

The sixth mechanism of thought reform Lifton describes as "loading the language."[29] Complex human problems are defined in brief, highly reductive phrases, easily memorized and expressed. These become the start and finish of any ideological analysis. In religious orders, these clichés and definitive-sounding phrases were used over and over again. For example, "holy obedience," "holy will of God," "sacred silence," "holy habit," "sacred voice of the superior" are phrases which both expressed respect for given ideas and things and reinforced attitudes toward them in the group. Sharing an in-group language also functioned to reinforce feelings of belonging and group solidarity.

The seventh instrument of thought reform is that of "doctrine over person."[30] Experience becomes much less important than doctrine and dogma. In religious orders the whole notion of self and religious experience was derogated or made subject to the notion of truth. The criterion of truth became dogma. Frequently, nuns became distant, disaffiliated from self, almost as if they were independent of their own actions and attitudes. Through formal teachings, spiritual reading, and meditation, nuns were repeatedly exposed to such phrases as "loss of self," "selflessness," "emptying oneself to be filled by God." Psychologically the result was that frequently the person lost a general identity and replaced it with dogma and doctrine.

The eighth theme of Lifton's scheme is that of the "dispensing of existence."[31] The totalist environment defines those who have a right to exist and those who do not. In religious orders, it is not the dispensing of existence itself that is at stake, but rather the definition of good and bad people, worldly people and saints, believers and nonbelievers—in short, those who are saved and those who are damned.

Lifton admits that no milieu ever achieves complete totalism but that many modern environments show some signs of it. The one element which perhaps kept religious orders from being completely totalist institutions was the fact that membership was voluntary. The member chose to commit herself to the institution and decided to remain. However, this is misleading. A Catholic girl trained by nuns often saw the sacrifice and challenge of religious life as attractive. When she entered the life, the thought reform processes were so intense and imbuing that it is doubtful whether one can speak of "complete freedom."

In summary, pre–Vatican II religious orders can be described as utopian groups, isolated from mainstream society in order to maximize the goal of total dedication to living out the central myth of Christian theology. In order to achieve this goal, the behavior of members was highly controlled. By the regulation of contacts between members and the outside world, control over values, attitudes, and thought patterns of members could be more effectively achieved and oriented toward daily living out the myths which legitimated the existence of the group.

Post–Vatican II Religious Orders

While it is relatively easy, because of their homogeneity, to characterize religious orders in general prior to the council, to portray a general picture of orders since the council is more difficult because of the varying paces at which orders responded to the council's call for self-evaluation and adaptation. In order to demonstrate the kinds of changes that occurred, the case of one religious order will be presented in detail. The order described here is known later in this study as Order A, the change-oriented order, which was one of the three case studies. This order was one of the first in the United States to convoke a general meeting to consider how it would respond to the council decree on renewal. The order concomitantly effected some of the most widespread changes in the country. Since this order effected change in 1968–1970, many orders have followed the same general pattern so that today this order does not stand alone as unique or extreme in the process of renewal. By using this change-oriented order, the nature and extent of the changes being introduced in religious orders in this country can be focused upon more distinctly.

History

Order A was founded in Ireland in the early nineteenth century. A young Irish woman and her companions had cared for victims of a cholera epidemic in Dublin, and, after the epidemic had subsided, they decided to remain together and dedicate themselves to Christian service. Later they felt called to journey to America to work as educators. After ten years of teaching in the East, the founder moved with her then expanded group of women to carry on her educational endeavors in the vast missionary expanse of the midwestern United States. Pioneers were just beginning to settle in the area, and the group caught their spirit of daring and adventure. Even today the congregation is known for its pioneering and bold character.

From a small group, the congregation grew until it numbered over 2,000 persons in 1969. Early recruits came from Ireland as a result of periodic trips made there by sisters in the order to solicit members. Increasingly, however, American girls requested to enter the order. Most of these girls had attended schools taught by the sisters. By the mid-1960's the order had expanded its educational service so that members taught in congregationally staffed colleges, high schools, and elementary schools. In addition, pupils were being instructed in catechetical centers and vocational schools under direction of members of the order. The educational institutions in which members worked were spread out over the United States.

Order A was founded to impart Christian education and instruction to people in need of such services in any part of the world. The former constitution of the order specified the spirit in which such education should take place: "Each Sister shall imbue her pupils with the principles of the true faith and shall train their hearts to love God by the most diligent practice of all virtues; thus, while sowing in their minds the seeds of knowledge, she may unite their souls to God by fervent love." The sisters were instructed to give special attention to the virtues of charity, simplicity, and humility, which were the characteristic virtues of the congregation, and to attempt to instill these virtues in the hearts of those they taught.

In addition to these central virtues that characterized the order, there was a pervading spirit of adventure and individuality that dated back to the early members who pioneered new territories to teach. Even today, it is common to hear members talk about the boldness and courage of their early sisters and to compare the challenge of the present era in the church with that of the founding days of the order. For example, in a speech to the order, the superior general acknowledged this pioneer spirit as a gift from the foundress. "The spirit of our foundress, I remind you, was the spirit of an American pioneer. Once again we are pioneers, and in the spirit of pioneers we must move forward with hope to new frontiers."

The spirit of adventure and pioneering, no doubt, is one reason that Order A forged ahead in the renewal movement after Vatican II. Members were well aware of the story of their early founding and of the courage and daring demanded of their foundress. A spirit of forging ahead into new areas and taking the risks of uncertainty was instilled into the members as part of their heritage. When the challenge of change and renewal sounded forth from the council, this spirit was called forth and applied to the new frontiers opening up in religious life.

Change and Renewal

The members in Order A, during their renewal chapter in 1968, reviewed every aspect of their order. Instead of rewriting the constitution or drafting a new one, they compiled a book of guidelines or norms for the order. Before Vatican II, the order's constitution was known as the "rule book." The rules and regulations indicated in rule books had a sacred quality since they were sanctioned by Rome and were seen as means of sanctification of the members. In many renewal chapters, including the one held by Order A, the meaning of a constitution changed from that of rules established for members of the congregation to guidelines that express or reflect how sisters in that particular order live their lives. Instead of a constitution or rule book, many religious orders, in an attempt to indicate changes in meaning, began to refer to their renewal chapter decrees as guidelines or norms for renewal.

The guidelines that resulted from the renewal chapter in Order A begin with a series of statements on the nature of religious life, defining the meaning and purpose of being a religious woman in the modern church. To quote an opening statement:

> Today's religious, in responding to the spirit of renewal, concern themselves with witnessing to Christ in community. The forming of a truly Christian religious community demands the best of each person and promises Christlike humanness and penetrating vital experience of the Trinity's own personal life of communication in love . . . To realize community, barriers must be broken within ourselves, in others, and between others. This demands sensitivity, generosity, tact, respect and patience to build communication between those with whom we live and work. However, as religious we cannot limit such relationships to those who are near us. Our task is to make Christian community in the world.

Central ideas and norms that permeate the renewal guidelines are those of community, communication, and witness in the world. The hierarchical notion of superior and inferior was replaced with that of dialogue and communication among all groups and individuals in the order, and the stress on cloister and isolation from the world was replaced with that of availability and service to secular society. With the stress on greater association with nonmembers and less emphasis upon cloister, religious orders no longer concentrated on what Lifton outlined as milieu control. As discussed earlier, Lifton maintained that the basic feature of a thought reform environment is the control of human communication. Once this control is lost it becomes very difficult, if not impossible, to create and sustain total commitment to one world view. This, in fact, is what happened in religious orders. As nuns began to associate with members outside the order, many broadened their perspective and reference groups. It became more difficult to sustain a homogeneous world view among members.

The new governmental structure proposed and accepted by the renewal chapter provides for the "institutionalization of the cooperation of all members in discovering and serving the will of God (i.e., the needs of man)." The new governmental system of the order was aimed at a more broadly based, democratic structure of government with built-in lines to facilitate and "institutionalize" trust.

The new system of government was based upon two basic principles: collegiality, namely, participation in decision making by those who will carry out the decisions, and subsidiarity, the right of lesser and subordinate bodies to perform functions and make decisions of which they are capable. It was in the senate that the members of the renewal chapter saw the best example of the principle of subsidiarity. The senate was a body of sisters elected at large as well as the chairmen of working commissions which would present to the decision-making body programs and proposals from the "grass roots." The guidelines state that "this steady influx of sisters from the grass roots level will encourage fresh messages from the Spirit to the law-making body charged with the task of continual renewal."

The principle of collegiality was built into the local house structure since every house meeting was to "have the flavor of a town meeting." Regional representatives were to tap the local houses for creative ideas, spread them, and look to regional meetings to highlight and solve common problems. A board of appeals was established with the task of listening to the Spirit through those who have not been able to communicate their specific needs in other ways. In other words, a structure was set up to insure that every person would have a means to be heard.

The section on governmental changes in the guidebook ends with the statement that "the words 'experimental, evolutionary and self-correcting' emerged as a kind of touchstone for the new government." The notions of flexibility, openness to change, and responsiveness to historical pressures are characteristic of renewal in the order and diametrically opposed to the pre–Vatican II approach of stability, doctrinal certitude, and obedience to the one authority of Rome.

The principles of collegiality and subsidiarity militate against the mystical manipulation that Lifton describes as characteristic of obedience in totalistic environments. No longer is the word of the superior accepted as a manifestation of God's will. Rather, obedience is defined in strictly human terms, that is, as "openness to one another."

A keynote paper presented to the renewal chapter was entitled "Person, Freedom, and Responsibility." Throughout the chapter, the paper served as a theoretical basis for the discussion of many structural issues. The principal theme of the paper was that future religious community requires the development of persons able to make mature judgments and that for this personal freedom is essential. In commission reports and papers that followed, the community was seen as providing resources for the development of mature, responsible, religious women. "In order to place the consideration of our community resources, both personnel and finances, in the proper focus, it is necessary that we permeate our perspective with respect for the individual person and the recognition of her maturity, generosity, and responsibility to the corporate person of the community.'' Emphasis throughout the section was placed on the priority of the person and her relationship to the corporate person of the community. This emphasis reverses the earlier tendency to place doctrine over person. Once again, one of the indoctrination mechanisms Lifton describes and which characterized pre–Vatican II orders gives way to a personally oriented perspective.

In regard to the matter of dress, the chapter allowed sisters to wear whatever they felt was appropriate for their work. Rather than stipulating any one form of dress, the chapter instead formally stated that sisters wishing to retain the traditional habit would receive full support for this choice, and those sisters so choosing might wear contemporary dress. Veils were also optional. Those who desired that external symbol would receive support for wearing it, and those who wanted to wear a pin, pendant, or ring could select the one they preferred. This statement also indicated that those who preferred no external sign of their religious dedication would not have to be so identified. The practical result of this changed norm was that the sisters of Order A would no longer be necessarily identified externally as celibate, religious women.

The formal statement regarding communal prayer is very clear: ''The frequency with which sisters engage in any form of communal prayer should be determined by those who intend to participate . . . the group decides on the time and place for prayer which will best provide an atmosphere of calm, even in the midst of considerable activity.'' Instead of listing specific exercises of piety, the guidelines encouraged such prayer as Eucharistic celebration, mental prayer, common meditation on a rosary mystery, Scripture services, and the communal celebration of the sacrament of penance. Culpa, or the public confession of transgressions, gave way to a much more positive approach, namely, emphasis upon God as Forgiving Father. No longer is the community seen as providing a ''purging milieu'' for the sinner; rather, the community supports the person and offers reassurances.

While the renewal chapter encouraged greater collegiality and concern for the individual sister's choices regarding her job assignment, it was in the 1970 senate meetings that the most explicit and far-reaching changes were made. A proposal was passed introducing complete open placement into the congregation. The open placement structure meant that the responsibility for finding and maintaining a job was the individual sister's. The responsibility of the congregation was to assist her in that process by advertising job openings that came to the central administration and channeling the sister to schools and agencies where she might find the type of job in which she wanted to serve the church and society. No longer, then, was the sister in Order A to be placed in a parochial school or hospital by the superior, who indicated the "will of God" for the sister. The sister herself was given the responsibility of ascertaining what her talents and abilities were and in what capacity she felt the Spirit asked her to use them.

Structural changes in the order were reflected in the daily lives of the members. The manner in which the nuns spent their days differed from the daily routine in pre–Vatican II orders. For example, a typical day for one group of six nuns living together in Order A began with each member choosing her own time of rising, dependent upon the type of work she was doing and her personal body rhythms. Each person prepared and ate her breakfast when and if she wanted. The three who taught in the same parochial school went to work together in a common car. However, one of the remaining three was involved in religious education work in an inner city parish, one did social work in a city agency, and one was a nurse in a local clinic. While the nurse rode the city bus, the other two were provided cars.

Because of the varied activities associated with different jobs, it was unusual for all six to be home together for the evening meal, even though the group was continually aiming for this goal. One evening a week, however, everyone made a special effort to be home in order to celebrate Mass together. The parish priest, or occasionally a priest friend of one of the nuns, would come to the nuns' home and say Mass around the dining room table. There was much liturgical participation on the part of all present, both through singing and a dialogue sermon during which each person was invited to share ideas. Following Mass, the nuns would have dinner together. Because it was the only time during the week when the community gathered together for a communal activity, the evening was considered central to the solidarity and community spirit of the group.

Once a year each nun submitted a personal budget to the congregation. Each local group as well submitted a house budget, including such items as food and rent. As each nun received her monthly salary check, she retained what she had budgeted personally, gave to the local community what it had budgeted, and sent in the remainder to be used for a group retirement plan, to care for those members who were unable to work, and to cover operating expenses of the congregation. The nuns no longer depended on a communal shelf for clothing and personal articles but bought their own clothing from department stores of their choice.

Visits with family and friends were no longer limited to specified

Table 1. *Order A, 1958 and 1970*

Characteristics	1958	1970
Government	Superior general administers; assigns members to jobs and houses; assures uniformity in dress, furnishings, and customs. Her voice seen as will of God by sisters; local superiors share in authority.	While president administers, all sisters cooperate in discovering and serving the needs of man. Principles of collegiality and subsidiarity characterize every level in the order; Spirit speaks in all members, not just superiors.
Job assignment	Superior general determines what members are to do, where, and how. Receiving an assignment is receiving God's will in holy obedience.	Open placement puts responsibility for job on the individual. The order is to assist the person; the person herself is to discern where the Spirit is directing her.
Relation to externs	No one may have any associations with externs without explicit permission. Sisters go out by twos, never alone. All incoming and outgoing mail is opened and may be read. Never may sisters be alone with men unless the door is open.	Task of religious is to make Christian community, not only with other religious but in the world. Barriers that separate religious from the world hinder creation of community; religious women should be available to serve people wherever there is need.
Prayer	Detailed exercises of piety outlined in constitutions and mandatory for all in the order. Superior's responsibility to see that religious exercises are minutely carried out in the spirit of prayer. Punctuality and religious decorum during prayer are stressed.	Frequency, place, and type of communal prayer to be determined by the local group.
Dress	Uniform long habit and veil are carefully described in constitutions, and superiors are to see that no deviations from minutest details are allowed. Habit is considered "holy."	Each individual may wear what she wishes in regard to dress, veil, and any external symbol of her religious consecration.

times. Rather, the nuns were encouraged to spend time with their families whenever they could work it into their schedules. Family members and friends were also allowed to visit in the local convent. Even male relatives sometimes stayed overnight in the guest room. No longer were any areas designated "sacred" or "cloistered" as they were in pre–Vatican II convents.

The nuns frequently attended meetings, concerts, movies, and parties in the evening as well as during the day. It was not unusual for any one of the six to be out alone at night. Travel, both within the city and out of town, was part of the nuns' routine activities. They were now free to travel alone and were allowed to stay in hotels as well as in private homes.

Table 1 summarizes the kind of changes that occurred in Order A during the renewal process of the 1960's. In general, by 1970 Order A was radically restructured for the purpose of more effectively witnessing the gospel of Jesus Christ in the world and, in the light of that gospel, serving the needs of the people. The fundamental principles of collegiality and subsidiarity assured that the individual would have greater voice in the decisions of the congregation; a commitment to personal freedom and responsibility meant that the individual would choose her own job, where and with whom she wanted to live, and the type of dress and external identification that she preferred. The role of the congregation was to provide resources and challenges to the individual to make her choices in the light of a religious dedication and desire to serve the needs of people. Order A as well as many other religious orders during the latter 1960's changed from an isolated, highly routinized, and closed organization, characterized by mechanical solidarity,[32] to a structure resembling other voluntary organizations in which members, diversified in many aspects of their lives, join together to achieve a goal which any one of them would find difficult alone. Emphasis within religious orders changed from likeness among members to increasing diversity in all areas of daily life.

In the process of adapting and becoming open to the world, convents restructured many of the mechanisms which previously functioned to achieve a totalistic world view. Emphasis upon thought reform and a central unifying myth gave way to a philosophy of personalism and individual freedom of thought. Chapter two describes some of the unanticipated consequences of these changes.

2. Sociological Perspectives

Chapter one outlined the types of changes that occurred in religious orders in the relatively short span of a decade. This chapter will focus upon some theoretical perspectives which I hope will help in understanding what was going on organizationally. The hypotheses that are presented toward the end of the chapter arose out of these sociological perspectives. A brief methodological section describes how the hypotheses were tested empirically in the study.

It is important, first of all, to locate convents among the numerous types of organizations described in sociological literature. This enables us to pinpoint the unique characteristics of convents and their similarities with other organizations.

Utopias: Do Religious Orders Qualify?

Religious orders can be considered utopian organizations even though they have some characteristics that differ from most such groups. In *The Joyful Community*, Benjamin Zablocki utilizes the definition of utopias that was formulated by The Fellowship of Intentional Communities in the 1950's: "An intentional community is a group of persons associated together (voluntarily) for the purposes of establishing a whole way of life. As such, it shall display to some degree, each of the following characteristics: common geographical location; economic interdependence; social, cultural, educational, and spiritual interexchange of uplift and development. A minimum of three families or five adult members is required to constitute an intentional community."[1] I find this description one of the most succinct in the literature because it focuses upon structural characteristics of such groups as well as upon purpose and values. Zablocki uses the term *intentional community* rather than *utopia* in order to avoid the value loadings frequently associated with such words as *utopian community, utopian ideals*, *communistic society*, or *cooperative colony*. Throughout this book, the above description of a utopia or intentional community is utilized. The two terms *intentional community* and *utopia* are used synonymously.

In his review of recent books on utopian groups, Jesse R. Pitts adds a new dimension, or emphasis, to the definition quoted above: namely, that a utopian community is dedicated "to the realization in the everyday life of its members of a higher level of value achievement than is apparently present in the society at large."[2] Maren Lockwood Carden, in her analysis of Oneida, also stresses the importance of values in her definition of a utopia as an organization "founded specifically to implement in its social structure a particular set of ideals."[3] The purpose of a utopian community, therefore, is to organize around a value system, whether it be as explicit as the Bruderhof's radical, fundamental Anabaptist Christianity described by Zablocki or as vague as some of the contemporary communes' commitment to the "counterculture." What differentiates a utopian community from other types of organizations, for example, a corporation or a church, is the centrality of commitment to a given set of values and a social organization that separates the group in its day-to-day living from mainstream society in order to achieve these values.

A utopia in which members are dedicated to religious goals is like a religious sect in that both are usually small groups in which members aspire to personal, inward perfection and direct personal fellowship with other members of the group.[4] In both types of group, members often stand opposed to "worldly" values. However, while sect members are not usually separated, physically or geographically, from society, a characteristic of utopias is that members do live together apart from society.

Religious orders of women in the Catholic Church, at least in their pre–Vatican II modality, can rightly be classified as utopian communities. This is true despite the fact that they intentionally and explicitly serve the interests of a wider church community and are part of a larger church structure. The two central purposes around which religious convents and monasteries have built their total way of life are service within the Catholic Church and being exemplary models of a Catholic way of life. The purpose of erecting barriers, not only geographical and physical (such as the dramatic convent gates depicted in *The Nun's Story*)[5] but also social and psychological, was to create a sufficient distance from society so that total devotion could be given to achieving these religious goals.

Boundary Maintenance and Ideological Totalism

As numerous sociologists studying utopias have pointed out, boundary maintenance is a central requisite for such groups. Clear delineation of who is "in" and who is "out" is achieved by creating a life-style in which members associate together in many aspects of daily living. Association with nonmembers is usually restricted both physically in terms of geographical isolation and social-psychologically through restrictions on social contacts.

Boundary-maintaining structures can be viewed as the organizational correlate of Lifton's first mechanism of thought reform, namely, milieu control. Lifton maintains that control of human communication is the primary requisite for successful thought reform. Through milieu control the totalist environment seeks to establish domain over not only the individual's communication with the outside (all that she sees and hears, reads and writes, experiences, and expresses) but also over communication with herself, that is, thoughts, feelings, judgments, desires. The most basic result of milieu control is the disruption of balance between self and the outside world. The person is deprived of the combination of external information and internal reflection which anyone requires to test the realities of her environment and maintain a measure of identity separate from it. Rather, the individual is called upon to make an absolute polarization of the "real," that is, the prevailing ideology, and the "unreal," that is, everything else.

Totalist organizations that aim to imbue every member with a prevailing ideology create boundary-maintaining structures to achieve this goal. Boundaries are those structures—physical, social, behavioral cultural, and psychological—which define a group, set it off from its environment, and give the group a clear, coherent reason for existence, thereby facilitating commitment on the part of members. As Rosabeth Kanter points out, a central problem for twentieth century utopias is constructing strong boundaries and creating a coherent group in an urban era of mass communication, easy mobility, and rapid social change. Strong communities, she maintains, are those that can generate and maintain commitment because of their adaptive solutions to boundary problems, while weak communities succumb to the "boundary-denying forces" in society.[6]

Boundary maintenance is a problem for all organizations in that every organization must have clear goals to which members may choose to be committed or not be committed, must know who belongs and who does not belong, and must establish some set of rules of behavior to govern relationships among members and between members and nonmembers. For utopian groups, however, which by definition demand a high degree of commitment from members and some degree of isolation from the larger society, the problem of boundary maintenance becomes primary.

One mechanism used by utopian groups for assuring a high degree of membership commitment is erecting strong boundaries so that constant competition for membership loyalties is diminished. By isolating members from the larger society, not only physically but socially and psychologically as well, the individual is protected from having to make constant decisions regarding her ties. At the same time that strong boundaries serve negatively to keep members from outside influences that might threaten their in-group loyalties, they also serve positively to reinforce the individual's need for the group since she must look to group members to fulfill her needs for meaning, acceptance, and social relationships, as well as physical needs of food, clothing, and shelter. Strong boundaries, therefore, tend to reinforce group solidarity and membership commitment to the values, goals, and norms of the group.

The central boundary-maintaining structure in religious orders is the requisite of celibacy, whereby the role involvements of an individual are limited. Robert K. Merton introduced the concept of role-set to describe the array of role relationships in which persons are involved by occupying a particular social status.[7] The idea of role-set is pertinent in the context of describing the celibacy of nuns because the explicit purpose of celibacy as it was established within religious orders was to "consecrate" or "set aside" an individual for exclusive service to God and the church. By requiring that a person renounce the psychological and social absorptions demanded by a spouse and family, the institutional demand of celibacy is a radical type of boundary-maintaining structure. Complete loyalty to the order is achieved by prohibiting any special ties to groups of individuals that might interfere with total religious commitment.

Utopias set themselves apart from the larger society in order to establish a whole way of life that supports the values constituting the reason for their existence. However, such organizations, isolated from the mainstream of life, can thrive, as Lewis Coser maintains, "only if they are able to absorb their members fully and totally within their confines. Whatever draws the member away from the community threatens it."[8] Threats to community are not only challenges from outsiders but also individualistic attachments within the community that can threaten its solidarity and the intensity of the person's commitment to the group.

Georg Simmel, an early twentieth century sociologist, maintained that in the modern world the individual lives at the intersection of many social circles. A person, he felt, is "determined sociologically in the sense that the groups 'intersect' in his person by virtue of his affiliation with them." Modern man is thus subject to the web of numerous pushes and pulls that his various group affiliations demand of him.[9] Primary among these demands are those made by spouse and family. By requiring that members in religious orders take a vow of celibacy, the stresses, strains, and commitment that family ties make upon the individual are eliminated and replaced by total dedication to service in the church. Celibacy, therefore, is one of the most effective means of creating total milieu control.

One function of celibacy in religious orders, therefore, was total and undivided concentration and commitment of members to Christ and his church. A related function was commitment to the religious order itself. As Philip Slater demonstrates, there has been fear and suspicion of dyadic intimacy in all social life and especially in small, closed organizations where loyalty to the group is essential to its continuation. Whatever draws a member away from total involvement to the community is a threat to its existence.[10] Sexual relationships constitute one of the most powerful potentials for very particular and private relations between individuals. Therefore, sexual relationships must be tightly controlled if a utopian community is to survive.

At first glance, no two things may seem so divergent as the complex sexual patterns in the Oneida community, whereby partners were constantly exchanged, and the celibacy of religious orders. However, as Lewis Coser points out, the function of both systems is identical, namely, to reduce conflicting role sets and divergent loyalties and to achieve greater commitment of the individual to the group itself.[11] Both structures therefore function to achieve the type of milieu control that leads to total commitment of the individual to the goals of the group.

Yonina Talmon, in her discussion of marriage in the kibbutzim, also points up vividly how marriage patterns function to enhance commitment to the group. Marriage between second generation members of the same kibbutz would proliferate kinship ties within the kibbutz. Therefore, second generation youth were encouraged to marry someone from another kibbutz who would be totally unrelated to them. Since the kibbutz is based on the primacy of membership ties over kinship affiliations, it cannot afford to let kinship gain an upper hand. Predominance of kinship ties over ties of membership undermines the primacy of collective considerations and engenders strife. One primary function, therefore, of encouraging marriage with someone of another kibbutz is to check the emergence and consolidation of large and powerful kinship groupings that would mitigate against total commitment to the larger group.[12] Not only celibacy, therefore, but all marriage prescriptions and proscriptions can be part of an organization's attempt to control the milieu so as to maximize commitment of the individual to the ideological goals of the group.

While celibacy has been an institutional requirement for clergy in the Western Catholic Church, at least since the fifth century, clerical celibacy has had constant threats in the history of the church. While Pope Gregory VII, the great eleventh century reformer, tightened control over the celibacy requirement by ruling that all confessions heard by noncelibate priests were invalid, thereby soliciting the laity in enforcing clerical celibacy, almost every period in church history since then contains a struggle to enforce celibacy in the priesthood.[13] One of the reasons for the difficulties of clerical celibacy is that diocesan priests do not live in community and do not experience communal supports for their radical commitment on an everyday basis. What differentiates religious orders of both men and women is that celibacy is institutionalized within a tightly cohesive group, isolated from the larger society and from social relationships with outsiders that might threaten the total commitment of members.

Besides the proscription of marriage relationships, another boundary-maintaining structure was the set of stringent rules regarding relationships between members within the order itself. "Particular friendships" were taboo, and no two members were to spend time alone together. No doubt, regulations regarding exclusive relationships arose partially from the fear of lesbianism within an all-female institution; however, the explicit rationale for such rules was to assure the development of community bonds rather than dyadic friendship ties. Just as members of the Shaker community were required to confess transgressions against such friendship restrictions and to report transgressions of fellow members, in religious orders public admission of "particular friendships" took place during culpa, or public confession ceremonies.

Isolation mechanisms, such as restrictions on contact with nongroup members, also served boundary-maintaining functions in religious orders. Contact with a member's family was highly regulated, and, when allowed, such visiting was limited to designated rooms of the convent.

Telephone calls were allowed only with permission of the superior, and all incoming and outgoing mail was censored. The explicit purpose of these regulations was to avoid temptation and influence from worldly sources and to emphasize mutual support and dependence among ingroup members. Similarly, in the kibbutz young people often travel many miles to attend regional secondary and vocational schools rather than associate with nongroup members in surrounding nonkibbutzim schools.[14]

The mechanisms used by religious orders to obtain membership commitment and an intense sense of ingroup solidarity were parallel to many of those used by other utopian groups, such as the Bruderhof or the Oneida community. The recruit went through a ritual death and rebirth of the self process much like that of the Bruderhof newcomer. During these processes emphasis was placed upon desocialization and eradication of all previous worldly habits and socialization into a new "world view" in which the individual's behavior and attitudes were integrated into a new perspective. This new orientation was then internalized and became part of the core personality of the recruit. Boundary maintenance within religious orders was therefore achieved not only structurally through regulations and physical isolation but also through psychological processes whereby the individual accepted and internalized the whole way of life. In this way, religious orders achieved the ultimate stage of milieu control, which Lifton describes as control over the individual's inner communication with himself or herself.

It is clear that in terms of their internal structures and day-to-day life-styles religious orders are indeed totalistic utopian communities. However, they do differ from most utopian groups that have been studied in that they are part of a larger institutional structure, namely, the Catholic Church, with all of its status hierarchies and systems of social control. Being part of a larger social institution is one of the primary reasons why religious orders have continued in existence for centuries while most utopian groups last only decades. While some groups, like the Shakers, Bruderhof, and Moravian communities, have lasted for as long as fifty to one hundred years, the majority of them in the United States are less than ten years old.[15] Unlike these other groups, the fact that religious orders service a community outside their own boundaries, depend on financial remuneration from these services, and are subject to control by church hierarchy cushions them against being dependent solely upon their own resources for subsistence and helps to insure long-term survival.

The very fact of their embeddedness within the larger church structure, however, serves as a double-edged sword. While it has helped in the past to insure continuity, it may be dysfunctional to the survival of orders in the post–Vatican II period. Responses to change initiated by the official church are leading to conflict, dissension, and disorganization in many orders today. While it has traditionally been possible to isolate members from society and reduce influence from ideas and values outside the group, it is hardly possible to shelter members from the influence of ideas originating within the church hierarchy itself.

Costs and Rewards of Membership

While Erving Goffman lists convents among his examples of total institutions,[16] there is one significant way in which convents differ from most of his other examples (prisons, mental hospitals, orphanages, army barracks). While membership in these groups is largely nonvoluntary, nuns do make a choice to join a convent and to continue their membership. Even though the voluntary nature of these choices may be diminished by social pressures and expectations, some degree of voluntariness remains. Because choice is involved, it is important to consider the costs and rewards of membership in religious orders.

Every organization has to build into its structures processes that reduce the rewards of other possible commitments and increase the rewards of commitment to itself. The individual member, in belonging to the group, gives up other options. Therefore, both costs and rewards are involved in being part of any group. When costs of belonging to a group outweigh the psychic and social advantages of belonging, the probability of the individual leaving the group increases. For example, in the "doomsday cult" in California which John Lofland studied, tensions and frustrations were great, especially in the early years as the group was getting established in the United States. However, converts were assured of a major payoff, namely, "of being virtual demigods for all eternity, beginning with a rule over the restored and reformed earth within the immediate future." Soon Sun Chang, Korean leader of the group, prophesied that in 1967 God would impose the millennium upon the earth and those who converted early would occupy the most favored positions in the new era. With the promise of such future rewards, sacrifices and frustrations were deemphasized.[17]

Commitment is both an organizational requisite and a personal orientation of the individual member. In this area of commitment to an organization there exists an interdependent link between organizational demands and individual rewards for remaining in the organization. For the group to obtain the kind of commitment it needs for survival, while fulfilling the needs of its members, demands organizational structures that ensure commitment by affecting people's orientations to the group. As Kanter shows, the core of commitment to a community is the relationship in which what is given to the group and what is received from it are seen by the person as expressing his true nature and supporting his self-concept. A committed person is loyal and involved and has a sense of the community being an extension of himself. Commitment, therefore, refers to the willingness of people to do what will help maintain the group because it provides what they need.

The structural requirement of celibacy, while very effective in creating loyalty to the group, is a radical form of social control based on an intense motivational commitment. Members in religious orders are not forced, either by coercive means or monetary incentives, to take the vow of celibacy. Rather, acceptance of a radical, celibate way of life is voluntarily chosen for the "sake of the kingdom." In Amitai Etzioni's typology of organizations, therefore, religious orders are normative institutions that rely on symbolic rewards and voluntary commitment for compliance.[18] However, celibacy represents a high cost, and one way of reducing that cost is for the system to be isolated from society and thereby to limit social relationships of the members to other celibate women in the order. In addition to reducing the cost of celibacy, such isolation reinforces positive rewards, such as the feeling of sharing in an intense ideological, religious commitment, the psychic reward of belonging to a dedicated group, and elite status in the Catholic Church because of a singlehearted dedication to God and his people.

Traditionally, in the Catholic Church, members of religious orders have held a privileged status in the hierarchical system and have been accorded high esteem by the laity in the church. The title sister has meant not so much a familial equal but a "helper" who is special and held in high regard because of her unique relationship to the supernatural. The exalted status of nuns in the church was buttressed by a theology which taught that religious life was a "higher state" than the lay state and made one a "spouse of Jesus Christ." Nuns, therefore, received the kind of respect from laity in the church that is usually reserved for sacred persons and objects.

The mystery created by being set apart from society by convent walls, the authoritarian and all-pervasive decision-making process, the highly routinized and sacrificial character of daily living, and the obedient and complete acceptance of this way of life by members added to the "above the ordinary" and "sacred" character of nuns. The whole utopian way of life, in this instance, gained an awe and respect from those in the larger church and even from outsiders. This esteem became, for the member of the religious order, a reward for the costs demanded of her by renunciation of family and the isolated life of the convent.

With the convocation of the Second Vatican Council by Pope John XXIII in 1962, changes, both theological and structural, were introduced into religious orders that affected every aspect of their social organization, including costs and rewards of membership. In the Second Vatican Council documents, one of the predominant themes throughout is the essential role of the laity in the church and the ''vocation'' of all Christians to witness to Christ. The documents deemphasize the exalted status of religious and put stress upon the call of every baptized and confirmed person to share in the ''priestly, prophetic, and royal office of Christ.'' The council fathers consciously attempted to reduce the status differences that typified groups in the church; however, by so doing, they unwittingly reduced some of the symbolic rewards that were previously associated with the role of nuns in the church.

The renewal process that occurred in religious orders in the aftermath of the council reduced many distinctions that existed formerly between religious and laity. In addition to change in garb, many rules and customs that prohibited association were changed. Night curfews, permissions to leave the convent, early rising hours, and visiting rules were changed so that religious women had more freedom to come and go as they wanted. Not only were regulations liberalized, but contact with seculars was positively stressed as the primary way in which the nun could fulfill her role and mission to be Christ to all persons. Post–Vatican II theology asked how the nun could be a witness to Christ cloistered behind walls that separated her from those who needed her witness. Cardinal Suenens' book, *The Nun in the World*, embodied this new theology and was read by almost every American nun in the early 1960's.

All these changes were made in the name of ''renewal'' and had as their explicit purpose the reduction of barriers between religious and the people they served. An unanticipated consequence, however, was that religious women began to realize that they were women as well as religious, and for many of them doubts regarding the value of their celibate life came into play.

One of the functions of the isolation mechanisms of pre–Vatican II orders was to limit the possibility of reference groups that might threaten the celibate commitment of members. A reference group is a person, or usually a group of people, that an individual takes as a frame of reference for self-evaluation and attitude formation.[19] Merton differentiates normative reference groups, which set and maintain standards for the individual, from comparative reference groups, which provide a frame of comparison relative to which the individual evaluates herself and others.[20] The physical and social isolation of the former system of convent life reduced the possibility of nonmembership groups becoming either normative or comparative reference points for the members in the order. One of the explicit functions of the cloister was to remove the person from contact with "the world" and its standards. The process of change from a cloistered style of life in which nuns were neither "in the world nor of the world" to a life-style where they were to be "in the world but not of the world" put religious women in contact with numerous nonmembership groups and increased the probability of any one of these groups becoming for her a salient reference group. Because of increased identification with reference groups other than celibate women, celibacy has become more costly and is no longer accompanied by the types of status rewards that existed before Vatican II.

As barriers, both physical and social, disappeared, so did the sense of "apartness" and "awe" with which laity in the church regarded religious. What had traditionally been status rewards disappeared, and no new reward system was introduced to make the remaining costs of celibacy worthwhile. The increase in the number leaving religious life after the council is one indication that many religious women no longer found membership in a religious order meaningful and worth the required costs.

Organizational Dilemmas

There are times in the life span of most organizations, just as in the life of individuals, when every solution to a problem entails costly consequences. Leadership in organizations, therefore, is constantly faced with cost and reward considerations in relation to policy making. Policy makers and administrators try to anticipate the costs and rewards of decisions. However, inevitably there will be consequences that are not anticipated, either in substance or in intensity.

Both Pius XII in his exhortations to superiors general in 1952 and the council fathers were concerned with making life within religious orders more meaningful to the members themselves and to the laity who come into contact with them. One reason for the renewal and updating of structures was to assure that young women would find life in religious orders rewarding enough to be willing to make the costs involved in giving up many satisfactions of a married or single lay life. The increasing numbers of women leaving convents was of concern to church officials, and they hoped that relaxing some of the ancient customs and demands of convent life would make it more attractive to contemporary young women. Ironically, however, some of the very changes that were instituted in order to make religious life less difficult for members and more in tune with contemporary conditions resulted in more and more members opting to leave religious orders.

One area that came under scrutiny in post–Vatican II years was the highly centralized, authoritarian governmental structure of religious orders. The council fathers mandated that every member in an order take part in the renewal process and that more democratic structures be instituted to assure the contributions that each individual member could make. The authoritarian structure in most orders was replaced by a more democratic system which encouraged greater personalism and individual initiative. Many of the routinized activities which traditionally carried with them connotations of "being obedient," such as being at prayer and recreation at designated times with the group, gave way to personal choice in these matters. An unanticipated effect in many orders was a loss of the sense of solidarity that such activities done in common achieved in the pre–Vatican II order.

As discussed in chapter one, the relationship between increased educational and professional preparation on the part of religious women and the concomitant structural changes brought about by more highly educated women also constitutes a central organizational dilemma for religious orders. Better educational backgrounds were necessary for nuns to be of service in accredited institutions. In order to meet standards for teachers, hospital personnel, and social workers, it was mandatory for orders to assure that their membership was qualified. However, in the process of preparing professional women for adequate service, many women became exposed to ideas and experiences which were an impetus for changes within the order and to increased numbers of women who decided they no longer wanted to serve as celibate nuns in the church and asked for dispensations from their religious commitment. Women who previously had little contact with nongroup members were suddenly exposed to alternative life-styles, and many of them opted for life outside the cloister.

Interestingly, the decline and breakup of the Oneidan community is traced by Carden to the time when John Humphrey Noyes, the founder, turned from the fervor of his earlier religious propensities to a preoccupation with the study of social science. While in the early days of Oneida Noyes insisted that the members spend several hours a day in religious study, discussion, and contemplation, he later encouraged "clubs for mutual improvement" and continuous self-realization of the individual. "Ironically," Carden says, "it was probably not the Community's inconsistent attitude toward its own religious principles but its consistently strong emphasis on education which allowed children to follow a somewhat different course from that taken by their parents."[21] All children were encouraged to read widely so they grew up with an appreciation of literary scholarship, with scientific training, and with at least a vicarious taste of the attractions of the outside world. In similar fashion, the training of nuns during the 1950's and 1960's and the "continuing education" programs for all members emphasized individual growth and self-realization. Group dynamic workshops and encounter sessions frequently replaced the traditional spiritual lectures and days of retreat that were customary in religious orders.

It is possible to summarize the changes that took place in religious orders as a result of the Sister Formation Movement and Vatican II as primarily changes in boundary-maintaining structures and in mechanisms that previously functioned to achieve solidarity and cohesiveness within the order. While the role requirement of celibacy remains unchanged, most of the structures that supported celibacy have changed. Since Vatican II, the convent walls have crumbled, and the structures that once separated religious women from the world are gone. Nuns today dress like their lay counterparts, work alongside of career and married women, choose where they want to work and with what members they want to live, have a degree of financial independence from the larger order, and in many instances are not recognized by their coworkers as nuns.

An organization that almost perfectly fit Goffman's description of a total institution became within the span of a few years, a type of voluntary organization where members join together loosely to achieve a common purpose. Goffman describes a total institution as "a place of residence and work where a large number of like-situated individuals, cut off from the wider society for an appreciable period of time, together lead an enclosed, formally administered round of life."[22] The normal barriers separating the sleep, work, and play aspects of life do not exist, and each phase of the members' daily activity is conducted in the company of many others who are treated alike. Decision making is highly centralized and encompasses the whole of the "inmates'" lives. While this model accurately describes pre–Vatican II orders, the life-style and structures of most contemporary orders more closely resemble a voluntary organization model where only a segment of a person's life is involved and where the organization is seen as a resource for the goals of the members.[23] The big question, however, that faces religious orders in the 1970's is whether they can adapt their goals and structures in such a way as to respond to the dilemma of better servicing the needs of contemporary society yet remain distinct enough to inspire membership commitment.

The intensity of the changes occurring in religious orders stems from the fact that not only their intermediate goals but the basic purpose for their existence is being challenged. When organizations face such crises, one option for survival is for them to redefine their goals, as the National Foundation for Infantile Paralysis did when the Salk vaccine was discovered and the organization's goal of combating infantile paralysis was achieved. In the course of meeting that goal, unique means were developed to gain membership involvement. The organization, therefore, in the face of the Salk crisis, redefined itself as something more than a special purpose association. Religious orders are presently in the throes of attempting to redefine and clarify goals.

A similar organizational dilemma faced the Moravian Brethren in Bethlehem, Pennsylvania, in the nineteenth century. The community began to participate in the emergence of an American nation and thus gradually moved from a religious enclave to a worldly, secular community. The institutions that had once attested to the dominance of the religious factor were replaced by economic, political, and social institutions of a purely secular character. Bethlehem, once a small, religious utopia where members were intensely committed to religious ideals, is today a "sprawling industrial city" with a population of over 75,000 and an economy tied to one of the corporation giants in the American steel industry.[24] Will religious orders follow a path similar to that of the Moravian Brethren of transforming their values and structures into a secular organization? Or can they adapt to the radical changes that they are experiencing in such a way as to maintain a religious character? Or will religious orders become a matter of historical record?

One of the critical organizational dilemmas facing religious orders in this period of change and transition involves the increasing numbers of members who are reconsidering their organizational commitment and leaving religious orders. At the same time, fewer persons are joining the orders so that maintaining membership has become an important organizational problem. In the previous system, a life commitment was made to the order and dispensation from this commitment was uncommon. In the past eight to ten years, however, many religious women who once made a permanent vow to the order have questioned their commitment and obtained ecclesiastical permission to sever their membership with the order and return to a lay life. Since religious orders are normative institutions and rely solely on membership commitment for continuance, how many people leave and who they are constitutes one of the central issues that will determine the future of religious orders. If large numbers continue to leave each year, and if the trend toward few new members persists, it is possible that religious orders constitute a dying institution in society. This raises the theoretical question of how much articulation and what types of association a utopian group can have with the larger society without losing the distinctiveness and solidarity of the group.

The present study is an analysis of the patterns occurring within religious orders of women in the United States regarding membership, with particular focus upon the relationship between the organizational changes occurring and membership losses. Since changes have been introduced into religious orders at different rates, and since orders vary in such characteristics as size and education level of members, it is possible to analyze relationships between rates at which members are departing and other organizational variables. Is change, in fact, associated with increased membership losses? How does increased educational preparation affect both change in an order and loss of members? Through empirical analysis the theoretical ideas in this chapter will be tested in the chapters that follow.

Hypotheses

In the previous section I discussed the fact that utopian groups are built upon the requisite of strong commitment of members to the ideals and values of the group. In order to achieve such commitment, utopias establish various types of boundary structures which set the group apart from the larger society and encourage strong in-group identity and solidarity. The changes that occurred in religious orders after Vatican II were primarily changes in boundary regulations such that increased contact of members with outsiders was not only allowed but given theological and apostolic support.

The present study hypothesized that structural changes in religious orders resulted in the lessening of personal commitment to the order on the part of many members. As contact with seculars increased and as greater individual freedom and decision making were encouraged, members became more aware of alternate life-styles and began to reevaluate the costs and rewards of a celibate religious life. Many of them opted to leave the group.

The operational definition of membership commitment used in this study was the number of women who choose to stay in an order compared with the number who choose to leave the group. In other words, the study focused upon the most general, but also the most radical, of commitment measures, namely, remaining or not remaining a member. Differences in degree of commitment on the part of members who stay were not considered.

Various questions regarding change and rates of leaving were of particular interest in the study. Is organizational change, in fact, related to increased rates of membership loss, that is, to the lessening of commitment on the part of members? Does structural change in religious orders follow a pattern such that a sequence of change can be predicted? Are increased educational levels in a religious order associated with structural change or with increased rates of leaving? If so, is it those who are educated who are leaving? Then there were numerous questions about *why* nuns were leaving. Are reasons for leaving related to change in the order? Does increased education lead to questioning one's commitment? Why are other women remaining in religious orders and who are they?

The present study combined a variety of methodological approaches to test empirically the above types of questions. Two hundred and eighty-seven orders responded to an organizational survey which included questions on changes in the order and the number of women who left the group each year between 1960 and 1970. Comparative analysis was done relating characteristics of the orders, especially change-related characteristics, to rates of leaving during the eleven-year period. One part of the study, therefore, focused upon organizational variables. The following hypotheses were tested with this organizational data.

HYPOTHESIS I: *Orders that have introduced more structural changes in the direction of greater decentralization and personal freedom are receiving fewer new members than orders that have introduced fewer or no changes.* In the pre–Vatican II era the sacrifice of the opportunities and enjoyments of secular life to seek admission to a religious order was a challenging "call." To surrender one's worldy attire for the uniform of a "candidate" and to place oneself under the direction and commands of a superior was dramatic and afforded a sense of sacrifice and mission for the sake of a higher goal. The new recruit also entered a privileged status in the church and was no longer regarded as simply a lay woman. In post–Vatican II orders, there is nothing to publicly identify a new recruit, and the sacrifices and renunciations demanded of her are far less noticeable than formerly. Even though the present new recruit lives in a convent or house of formation, during her first year or two she dresses in lay clothes and either goes to college or works in a regular job where she probably is not identified as "different" in any way. The status rewards associated with her new role are very minor, and yet she is forbidden to date or seriously associate with members of the opposite sex.

HYPOTHESIS II: *Orders that have effected more structural change in the direction of greater decentralization and personal freedom have lost more members than orders not having experienced such radical change.* In a utopian group where dedication to a value orientation is intense and all-pervading, it is crucial to maintain a sense of group solidarity and meaning. When a utopian community with a highly centralized authoritarian structure, such as existed in pre–Vatican II orders, moves rapidly to an open, more personally oriented system that resembles other voluntary organizations, the result is frequently a loss of the sense of group solidarity and legitimation for any remaining costs of group membership. In religious orders, where celibacy still remains a high cost, the democratization and personalization of lifestyle lead to emphasis upon the person and her needs and gifts. If, concomitantly, there is not great stress upon rewards and advantages of remaining a group member, the probability of members leaving the group increases.

HYPOTHESIS III: *Orders with higher levels of education lost more members than orders with lower levels of education.* The impetus of the national Sister Formation Movement was to better educational backgrounds and professional expertise of religious women. However, it had the unanticipated consequence of affecting boundary-maintaining structures such that religious women, in the process of being educated, came into contact with both thought systems different from and often contrary to those in their orders and also a variety of people who could become salient reference groups for them. As a result, nuns began to reevaluate costs and rewards of membership, and many decided that the costs were too high.

In addition to a national organization survey of religious orders, a sample of women who left three selected orders, each order having experienced differing degrees of structural change, was interviewed. The interview focused upon *why* the person left, what events or situations initiated her decision-making process, and what finally influenced her actual decision to seek ecclesiastical dispensation from her vows and the order. While this part of the research design centered on individual data, the person was studied in the context of the order from which she left. Organizational data, therefore, especially regarding degree of structural change, provided contextual data for studying individuals. The following general hypothesis was primary throughout this aspect of the study.

HYPOTHESIS IV: *Reasons women left their religious orders were related to the degree of change that had been effected within their orders such that there existed intragroup similarity in reasons for leaving and intergroup differences.*

In addition to this general hypothesis, the three following predictions were made regarding the types of differences in reasons for leaving that would characterize women from each of the three orders.

HYPOTHESIS V: *Many women who left the most change-oriented order left because they questioned the very meaning and value of religious life in the mid-twentieth century.* Within liberal orders more goal-related questions were being asked at the organizational level than in orders reluctant to change. Therefore, members in liberal orders were exposed more consistently to questions which related to the very legitimation of the institution.

HYPOTHESIS VI: *A greater number of women who left the least change-oriented order left because of dissatisfaction with the pace and directions of renewal in the order than was true for women who left the most change-oriented order.* The official church had not only suggested but mandated renewal and updating, thereby legitimizing change. Within those orders where change was not so readily accepted by the administration, frustration built up in the membership. Leaving the order could easily be justified on the basis of nonresponsiveness of the administration to the official church.

HYPOTHESIS VII: *Women who left the moderate-change order left because of personal reasons rather than reasons directly related to change or the lack of it in the order.* In the order that effected change slowly and systematically, members had opportunity to be part of the change process. They were challenged to reevaluate their commitment and to reexamine their motivation to be in the order. In the process, some women realized that they were not satisfied and would not be happy regardless of what the order did.

These seven hypotheses served as guidelines for the analysis of the data to be presented in the following chapters. However, before proceeding to a presentation of findings, it is necessary to discuss briefly the methodology used in the study.

Methodology

The present study utilizes three types of variables: global characteristics of religious orders, aggregate data on the members within each order, and individual data deriving from interviews with women within the orders. The joint use of these different types of data was necessary to best answer the basic questions of the study. The first set of questions asks: what overall patterns exist in rates of leaving from religious orders in the United States during the 1960's? Are any organizational variables systematically related to varying rates of leaving? In particular, is there a relationship between degree of structural change in religious orders and rates of leaving? The answers to these questions demand an organizational analysis in which each religious order becomes one case and the total number of orders studied is the N in the analysis.

There is, however, a second set of basic questions which demands another type of analysis: Why are individuals leaving religious orders? Is there significant variation in reasons for leaving among individuals? Are there patterns in reasons for leaving among individuals in the same order and do these reasons differ significantly for individuals in other orders? Are reasons for leaving related to degree of change in the order? The answers to these questions require the use of individuals as units of analysis and organizations as contextual data.[25]

The process of developing the research design was an evolutionary one that was adapted as the initial research progressed. The original plan was to choose three religious orders, at differing stages in the process of renewal and change, and to select a sample of interviewees from each in an attempt to study whether reasons for leaving and staying vary systematically depending on degree of change in the order. The possibility of obtaining some national organizational data on rates of leaving arose when I served as a consultant for a research project on religious orders in the United States sponsored by the Center for Applied Research in the Apostolate (CARA).[26] The project never materialized, but in the process of working with CARA it became evident that very little national data existed concerning the declining numbers of religious women. While consulting on the project, I came into contact with the Conference of Major Superiors of Women (CMSW), an organization which, a few months later, assisted me in conducting a national survey of religious orders.

Organizational Survey Data

The original design had emphasized individual interview data on why nuns were leaving, and organizational characteristics were seen as contextual background data. However, because of the unanticipated high response to the organizational survey, increased emphasis was given to organizational analysis as the study progressed.

Two surveys were sent to religious orders of women, the purpose of the second questionnaire being to supplement and clarify data from the first. During the 1960's some orders lost a relatively large number of their membership and, by 1970, were experiencing panic and anxiety in regard to their future. The issue of membership losses, therefore, was very sensitive in some orders. Several researchers, working with religious orders on less sensitive topics, predicted that a response rate of 30% would be very hopeful in the present project.

In order to maximize the probability of responses, some compromises were made on the first questionnaire, such as a less detailed question on numbers leaving. (See Appendix 1 for a copy of the questionnaire.) Interestingly, these warnings and precautions were unnecessary; with the first mail-out in June, 1971, to 430 orders in the United States, there was a return of 54%. A follow-up letter increased the response rate to 63%.[27] Enclosed with many of the returned questionnaires was a request from the administrators of the orders for data from the study which might assist the order in reducing the number of membership withdrawals. Several superiors general expressed gratitude that a systematic study of religious orders, especially regarding the increased numbers who were leaving, was being conducted. No doubt, also, the fact that the researcher was herself a member of an order made a difference in administrators' willingness to cooperate. As one superior general said, "It is so great that one of our own is qualified to do such a study from which we will all benefit." Many returned questionnaires included a personal note of encouragement.

The higher response rate on the mail survey and the interest of the administrators encouraged me to send out a supplementary questionnaire the following November in which additional data on the order was obtained and more detailed questions on rates of leaving were asked. At the same time, the first questionnaire was sent again to those orders that did not respond the first time. The second effort raised the response rate to the first questionnaire to 66.7% (N = 287) of all orders receiving the questionnaire.[28]

The mail survey was sent to presidents or provincial superiors of religious orders of women in the United States. A mailing list was supplied by the Conference of Major Superiors of Women (CMSW),[29] a national organization whose membership consists of the presidents of 430 religious orders and provincial superiors. (See Appendix 4 for discussion of the representativeness of the sample.) The board of directors of the CMSW also endorsed the study and commissioned the president to write a letter to every major superior in CMSW, encouraging her to cooperate with the study. This endorsement and support, no doubt, influenced the high response rate to the survey.

The response to the second questionnaire was not as complete as the response to the first; however, 184 (42.8%) orders did respond to the second as well as to the first, while 103 orders responded only to the first questionnaire. Throughout this study, therefore, the N is either 287 (all those responding to Survey I) or 184 (those responding to both Survey I and II), depending on the type of data being used in the analysis. The first group, those responding only to the first questionnaire, is designated as Survey I, and the group responding to both questionnaires is designated as Survey II.

The organizational questionnaires utilized in the study are presented in Appendix 1. In addition to numerous items on organizational characteristics, such as date of founding, size, geographical location, median age of membership, and governmental structure, there were a number of questions relating to structural change in the order and the number of members who left each year between 1960 and 1971. Each of the latter two variables is a composite measure formed from a number of discrete items in the surveys.

It was predicted at the outset of the study that change in religious orders is a linear process, such that certain structural changes precede other changes in a predictable fashion. The rationale for the prediction is the fact that religious orders are a type of social system in which various parts work together for the accomplishment of a specific goal. Change in any one part of the system has its effects on related structures. Because orders were initially quite homogeneous and subsequently were exposed to common stimuli, such as Pope Pius' exhortations to superiors general in 1952 and the decree on religious life during Vatican Council II, it was considered highly probable that structural changes would progress in similar fashion within religious orders although at different paces.

Rather than anticipating the progression of changes, Guttman scale analysis was used to ascertain whether there exists a sequential order of changes and what the series of changes is. Guttman analysis, therefore, was used for two purposes: (1) to test the prediction of a linear progression in structural change in religious orders and (2) to construct a scale of degrees of structural change.

Each order was asked what changes it had effected in five areas: prayer regulations, choice of living situation, mechanisms for job allocations, dress codes, and regulations on how sisters' salaries were handled. There was also a question on degree of membership participation in government through committees and commissions; however, this question had to be discarded because of ambiguous wording. The five items were chosen for inclusion in the survey on the basis of familiarity with some of the central issues considered by renewal chapters, a previous case study by the researcher on a religious order, and suggestions from other researchers involved with studies of religious orders during renewal chapters. (See chapter one for the ways each of these items changed from pre–Vatican II orders to post–Vatican II orders.) Each item was weighed and used to form an index with values 0–4, with 0 indicating least change and 4 greatest change.

Analysis of the five change items for the 184 orders that responded to both surveys resulted in a Guttman scale with a coefficient of reproducibility of .90 when specific cutting points were used for each item. The minimum marginal reproducibility for the five items was .73, which is a .16% improvement and indicates the extent to which the coefficient of reproducibility is due to response patterns rather than the inherent cumulative interrelation of the variables used. The coefficient of scalability for these items was .62, which indicates that the scale is unidimensional and cumulative.

In most Guttman scale analysis, the sequence of items that form a scale are interpreted attitudinally, that is, if an individual "passes" an item or has a given attitude, he will also "pass" other items in the scale, if the scale is truly unidimensional and cumulative. Central to Guttman analysis is the requirement that items are scalable and ordinal such that each item can be divided into two portions, pass or fail, yes or no, and that the items be ranked such that passing one item is predictive of what other items will be passed or failed. In the case of organizational data, such as the change scale in this study, passing or failing items is interpreted as having or not having given structures. Each item, therefore, must have a cutting point; orders that pass the item have the structure and orders that fail do not.

The five change items were dichotomized as follows: (1) prayer structure: forms and times of prayer are uniform within the order, and prayer is determined by the local group; (2) living situation: individual is assigned to living community with no personal choice, and individual chooses where she wants to live under certain conditions; (3) job allocation: assignments of members to jobs or allowing them to apply for published positions, and job choice being the responsibility of the individual; (4) dress code: members must wear some type of prescribed uniform or habit and a veil, and members may wear contemporary clothes, sometimes of prescribed colors, and may be required to wear a veil; (5) financial structure: salaries are sent to a superior or to the sister who forwards the whole amount to a superior, and sisters receive salary, keep budgeted amount, and send in the remainder.

The following items comprised the final change scale and the number of orders that responded positively and negatively to each item:

	Yes	No
Form and content of prayer chosen by local community	103	49
Contemporary clothes worn	86	66
Sisters determine living situation under certain conditions	57	95
Sisters choose their own jobs	19	133
Sisters receive salary, budget, and turn in remainder to community	12	140

Analysis of the responses to the change items indicates that the underlying dimension of change in religious orders is greater individual choice, which results in a weakening of congregational uniformity. Orders find it easier to decentralize to the local community than to allow individual choice in certain matters. Moving from total uniformity in prayer forms to variety on the local level has been effected by 103 of the orders. When it comes to less uniformity in dress, placement of members in living situations, and allocation of jobs, there is greater reluctance, and when it is done there are usually restrictions on the amount of individual freedom. For example, while contemporary dress is allowed in 86 of the orders, in many of them there are restrictions on color and veil. The area in which least change has been effected is that of finances. Only 12 orders allow the individual any type of freedom in regard to her salary. Rather, financial matters are still highly centralized.

The five items were combined into a change scale ranging from 0 (most conservative) to 4 (most liberal). The percentage breakdown for orders that responded to both surveys is as follows:

scale score	% of orders
0	21
1	23
2	19
3	27
4	10

The above breakdown of scores shows that 44% of the orders scored conservatively on the change scale and 37% liberally, with 19% in the middle category.[30] There is sufficient variation in scores, therefore, to allow meaningful analysis of the relationship of degree of change to other organizational variables.

While change is defined empirically in this study in structural terms, that is, the degree to which central structures have been revised and "renewed," structural change is only one aspect of the changes religious orders are undergoing in this post–Vatican II era. Equally important, no doubt, and intertwined with the types of structural changes that have taken place are the attitudinal, ideological, and theological changes that led to and became the rationale for changes in structure. However, the structural changes are the ones which are most visible and can be measured most easily. Furthermore, the use of a measure of structural change is in keeping with the theoretical thrusts of the present study since it is hypothesized that the "liberalization" of certain regulations in religious orders leads to greater contact with the larger society and subsequent individual reevaluations of the costs and rewards of celibacy. Hopefully, however, later studies can expand the dimensions of change considered here in order to determine whether the same relationships between change and other variables are maintained when the conception of change is expanded.

Rate of leaving is also a composite measure computed in several ways: (1) in order to determine an average rate of leaving for the years 1960–1970, rate of leaving for each year was computed by taking the number who left in a given year and dividing by the total number in the order for that year; then, the 11 rates were added and divided by 11 to obtain an average rate for the 11-year period; (2) to determine a rate of leaving for all 11 years, the numbers who left during 1960–1970 were totaled, and that total was divided by the average size of the order for those years, calculated by adding the size for each year and dividing by 11. This measure is used most frequently in the analysis because the focus of the study is on the number who left during the decade of the 1960's rather than on those who left in each year of that period.

In some analyses, rate of leaving, calculated in the previous two ways, is based on the total number who requested either permanent or temporary releases, as indicated in Survey I; in most analyses, however, rate of leaving is based only on number who requested permanent dispensations. Unless otherwise indicated, rate of leaving refers to the more precise and conservative measure, that is, rate of leaving for those with permanent dispensations.

Case Studies

In addition to the organizational survey, three religious orders of women in the United States were chosen as case studies. A sample of individuals was then interviewed from each order. In the study, therefore, the three orders serve as contexts for analyzing data on individuals in each order. Throughout the book, *case study data* refers to the information gathered on each of the three orders. This data was collected by means of records, participant observation, and informal conversations with members. *Interview data* refers to the formal interviews conducted with the sample of members and ex-members.

The selection of the three orders was based on the following criteria: (1) degree of change in the order as judged by researchers working with religious orders throughout the country (the sample of orders was selected before the survey was administered so that survey data on degree of change was not available; however, the subsequent data confirmed the fact that each of the three orders was representative of varying degrees of structural change); (2) geographical location (within a 100-mile radius of Chicago); (3) teaching as the primary organizational purpose; and (4) a membership of at least 500. Since the key factor in this part of the research concerned the timing and degree of change, the design called for the selection of one order that had initiated change early in the renewal process and had effected substantial changes (Order A), one that began to effect change in the late 1960's and was still in the change process (Order B), and one that was only now beginning to effect change of any kind (Order C).

The superiors general of each of the three orders were contacted and asked if they would be willing to cooperate with the study by allowing research of the order itself and providing a list of people who had left the order in the past five years. The superiors general of Order A and Order B were not only willing to cooperate with the study but were eager to share in its results. The provincial head of Order C never gave a definite refusal but was very hesitant to allow research in the order. She did not want to provide a list of members who had left nor did she favor having the researcher interview within the order. Rather than pursue the request to the point of hostility or an irrevocable ''no,'' I compiled a list of people who had left from information given by several members in the order. In fact, ''leavers'' from this order were easier to locate and contact than leavers from either of the other orders because of the well-organized network they had formed. The majority of those who had left had settled around Chicago and Detroit and kept close contact with others who had left the same order.

Interview Data

Sample of ''Leavers''

A sample of sixty women who had left the three orders between 1965 and 1971 was selected, twenty from each order. Due to the difficulties in contacting several of the women, the final sample included nineteen from each group. Given the fact that certain background variables were important for the analysis, a quota sample rather than random sampling design was used. Interviewees were chosen using the following criteria as a basis for stratification: age, occupational background, year of leaving, educational preparation, academic fields, marital status, and position in the order before leaving. For all three orders, the majority were in their twenties or thirties; however, this simply mirrors the fact that the majority of ''leavers'' are in this age group. For each order, three or more were interviewed who were over forty.

The number of years interviewees were in the order ranged from less than 4 to over 25 years; the largest numbers were members from 5 to 15 years. From Orders A and C someone was interviewed who had at one time been in the administration and also someone who had participated in one or more general chapters. The fact that none of the ''leavers'' from Order B fell into these categories is in keeping with the fact that very few women in the administration had left. Many women in the sample had a M.A. and almost all had bachelor's degrees. A larger proportion of people left Order A after completing their doctorate degree than is true of either of the other two orders, and, therefore, great effort was made to include two women from Order A who had obtained a Ph.D. before leaving. No one had left Order C with a doctorate at the time of the interviewing, and the list that was provided by Order B also included no one with a doctorate among the "leavers." In order to determine whether reasons for leaving differed for women who had already made a permanent commitment from those with only a temporary one, some women from both groups were included for each order. Thus, fourteen interviewees had left before making a final and lifelong commitment to the order. About half of the women who left each group were still teaching in parochial school. Relatively few, in fact, changed occupations after they left. Only five from Order C did different work after leaving, four from Order A, and two from Order B.

Interviewees, with the exception of only two or three, were most cooperative and almost eager to talk. When the person was contacted by telephone to arrange an interview, she was given an overall picture of the study and told that a primary goal of the research was to find out from those women who had left various orders why they left and how they evaluate changes in religious life today. In addition, for two out of the three orders, it was possible to say that the superior general had provided a list of women who had left, thus assuring the interviewee that she was not betraying the order and that the superior general was aware of the study.

Personal interviews of approximately one hour were conducted with each of the "leavers." The interviews took place either in the home of the interviewee or in an office provided by a local college. An interview guide (see Appendix 2) was filled out as the interview proceeded, and the majority of interviews were taped. In a few cases, the interviewee objected to the use of a tape recorder, and in these instances no recorder was used.

Sample of "Stayers"

In addition to the twenty "leavers" from each order, a matched sample of ten who had remained in Order A and ten in Order B were interviewed. These ten were matched with the leavers on the basis of the criteria used to select the first sample. Therefore, there was variety within the sample of each order concerning age, occupation, educational experience, and academic field. Because of the lack of official cooperation from the nonchange group, only six persons were interviewed from Order C. Among these six, however, there was variability in regard to age, status in the community, occupation, and academic training.

The schedule used in interviewing those who were still in the orders contained the same general background questions as the questionnaire for leavers. However, instead of questions on reasons for leaving, interviewees were asked why they were choosing to stay (see Appendix 2).

This book, therefore, is based upon organizational survey data, case study material, and interviews, depending on the question being considered. Chapters three and four discuss relationships among change, rates of leaving, size of order, and levels of education within orders. Accordingly, the survey data is most appropriate. Chapter five focuses upon reasons some nuns are leaving and others are staying. At this point, the case study data and personal interviews are used most extensively.

3. Declining Membership in Religious Orders

Despite the fact that most utopian communities are short-lived, religious orders have been in existence for many centuries. The mechanism of permanent commitment which members are required to make after the stipulated period of time in religious orders has been one of their greatest organizational strengths and one explanation for their longevity. By permanent vows, members promise to live celibately, poorly, and obediently for life, according to the constitutions of their particular order. This requirement of permanent commitment under vow makes religious orders unique among utopian groups.

However, beginning in the early 1960's and mushrooming throughout the decade, the number of applications for dispensations from permanent vows increased significantly. More and more nuns opted to leave religious life and return to the secular world. At the same time, fewer new recruits were entering during the latter half of the 1960's. As a result, the numbers of personnel in religious orders diminished significantly during the decade. Figure 1 shows the total number of religious women in the United States for the years 1960–1976. In 1960, there were 168,527 religious women who were members of religious orders with motherhouses or provincialates in the United States. Until 1966 this number rose each year, with the exception of a slight decrease in 1965. 1966 was the peak year for religious orders, with 181,421 nuns in the United States. However, beginning in 1967 and continuing until the end of the decade and through the mid-1970's, the number of religious women decreased each year at a much more rapid pace than the gradual increase in the first half of the decade. By 1976 the total number had declined to 130,995, a decrease of 50,426 in the decade since the peak in 1966. This represents a 28% decrease since the peak number in 1966.

This decrease in the number of religious women is especially dramatic since demographically the "baby boom" cohort reached their teenage years during the 1960's and early 1970's. We could expect, therefore, on demographic grounds alone, that the number entering religious orders would have swelled in these years, just as high school

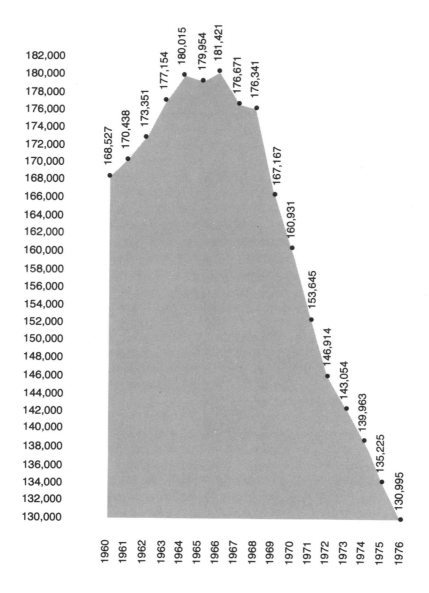

Source: *The Official Catholic Directory, 1960–1976.*

Figure 1. Changes in Number of Nuns in U.S., 1960–1976

Table 2. *Median age of membership by order and year*

N = 287

Median age	1960		1967		1970	
	No.	%	No.	%	No.	%
20–30	12	9	7	4	3	1
31–35	19	13	15	8	4	1
36–40	34	24	29	15	21	8
41–45	22	16	41	21	45	18
46–50	32	22	51	26	55	24
51–55	16	11	33	17	67	27
56–60	7	4	13	7	44	18
61+	2	1	4	2	9	3
No data	143	—	94	—	39	—
Total	287	100	287	100	287	100

and college enrollments mushroomed. The numerical decline of membership in religious orders is, therefore, accentuated by the increases in the population of women of entering age in those years.

This decrease in membership in religious orders after 1967 must be viewed from two sources simultaneously: (1) decline in numbers of women entering religious orders and (2) increase in numbers leaving the orders. Numerical changes in any institution result from these two sources plus the death rate of members.

While death rate data on religious women during the time period under consideration are not available in the present study, a question on median age in each order was included in the survey. Table 2 presents median ages in these 287 orders for three years, 1960, 1967, and 1970. Median ages in religious orders rose significantly between 1960 and 1970. In 1960, 16 percent of the orders had a median age over 50 years; by 1967 this figure rose to 26 percent, and by 1970 it reached 48 percent, or almost half of the orders. Given the fact that no unusual natural catastrophe occurred during the 1960's, it can be assumed that the death rate for religious women in the United States stayed relatively constant during that period. The decreases in total number of religious women, therefore, are explicable in terms of changes in the remaining two sources, numbers entering religious orders and numbers withdrawing their membership.

New Recruits into Religious Orders, 1960–1970

For the 287 orders that responded to the mailed survey, data are available on the number of individuals in the novitiate for three years, 1960, 1965, and 1970. The number of novices is used as a measure of the number entering the order rather than the number of candidates, postulants, or associates since prenovitiate status terminology differs from order to order while canon law requires a formal year of novitiate and prescribes duties and programs to be undertaken during that year, known technically as the "canonical novitiate year." In addition, the year of novitiate is formally the first step into a religious order, and it is at this time that the women receive religious names, take on the prescribed dress of the order, and begin to abide by the norms of the order's constitution.

In 1960 there were 10,272 women entering the 287 orders surveyed. By 1965 this number had dropped to 9,158, a numerical decrease of 1,114. By 1970 this number had dropped to 6,801, a numerical decrease of 3,471 since 1960. The decrease between 1965 and 1970 more than doubled the decrease between 1960 and 1965. During the latter period there was a change in entrance requirements in most orders that accounts, in part, for the decreasing numbers that entered since 1965. Previously, the majority of novices entered during or immediately after high school. The usual pattern was for the young girl to have attended a Catholic parochial school, to have been taught by a particular order of nuns, and to enter that order. Direct recruiting efforts were made by the order, usually in the form of talks or workshops given by a nun recruiter from the order. The Sister Formation Movement during the 1950's gave impetus to recruiting girls right out of grammar schools. High school programs, or aspirancies, as they were called, were established by most orders to provide both high school education and religious formation to girls who entered at that age.

With the stress of Vatican II on the necessity for an adult decision regarding the living of the three vows, religious orders reversed their entrance requirements and required that recruits have not only a high school diploma but also a college degree or comparable years of work experience. During the year or two that religious orders planned this program and revised their recruiting techniques, many orders did not accept applicants. This drastic change in recruitment rules explains, in part, the changes in numbers entering religious orders in the latter 1960's.

The probability of a young woman entering religious life after four or five years of college life or a career in the business world is far less

Table 3. *Number of new members by number of orders and year*

N = 287

| No. entering | 1960 | | 1965 | | 1970 | |
	No.	%	No.	%	No.	%
0	17	6	12	4	78	27
1–5	53	18	71	23	135	47
6–10	49	17	66	21	21	7
11–15	37	13	35	10	5	2
16–20	24	9	17	6	4	1
21–40	49	17	30	14	4	1
41–60	11	4	16	6	4	1
Over 60	47	16	40	16	37	14
Median	13		9		3	

than it is after high school, at age seventeen or eighteen. The type of program required to satisfy the intellectual and emotional needs of older women is vastly different from that demanded by a younger person. In regard to acceptance policies, religious orders were again faced with an organizational dilemma. It was felt that the challenge of religious life in the mid-twentieth century demanded older women who were more mature and experienced. However, by increasing age requirements, orders decreased the number of new recruits. They also began to recruit more independent women who were less easy to socialize to totally new ways of thinking and living. If the trend toward accepting only older, professionally prepared women continues throughout the seventies, as it probably will, it can be predicted that the smaller number entering religious orders will continue and that median ages will concomitantly rise.

Gross entrance figures for the country as a whole do not necessarily reflect trends in all individual orders; the question remains whether this decline is characteristic of all orders or whether some orders are gaining members while others are not recruiting successfully. Table 3, which presents data from the 287 orders that responded to the survey, shows the number of novices in each order for the three years 1960, 1965, and 1970. The median number entering dropped from 13 in 1960 to 3 in 1970. In 1970, 27% of the orders had no one in the novitiate. In this same year another 135 orders (47%) had between 1 and 5 new recruits, making a total of 213 orders or 74% having fewer than five new members. Comparatively, in 1960, 70 orders or 24% had fewer

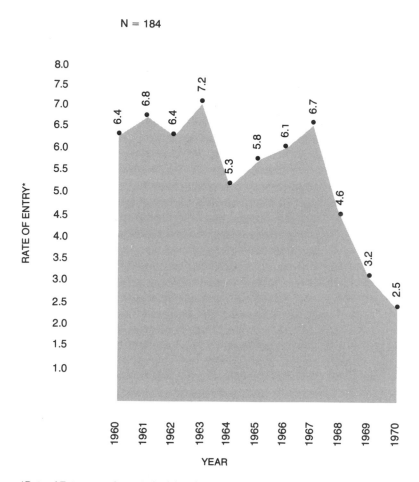

*Rate of Entry = number entering/size of order.

Figure 2. Mean Rate of Entry into Religious Orders, 1960–1970

than five novices, and in 1965, 83 orders or 27% reported fewer than five new members. In 1970 there were 143 more orders with fewer than five new members than in 1960.

Survey II asked for the number entering *each* year from 1960 to 1970, so that for each of these 184 orders, data are available for each of the eleven years. The size of many orders was decreasing throughout the decade because of increased numbers of nuns leaving. It is important, therefore, to take declining size into account when considering number of women entering. This is done by calculating a rate of entry. The number of new members accepted into an order can be viewed as a rate of entry by calculating the number of novices for a given year divided by the total number of members. If total size and number entering vary proportionately, the rate of entry would remain constant.

Figure 2 depicts graphically the trends in entry rates during the 1960's. The mean entry rate for the 184 orders was 6.4% in 1960, and it dropped to 2.5% by 1970. The highest rate occurred in 1963, 7.2%. In the following two years the rate dropped into the 5% range, and then in 1967 there was a slight increase again with a rate of 6.7%. After 1967 the rate steadily and rapidly decreased to its all-time low in 1970. The 1963 high corresponds with the close of the Vatican Council and the increased public attention to the promulgation of the council decrees. There was great anticipation and hope in religious orders for needed changes and the renewal of outdated structures. Also, 1967 was an optimistic year in most orders since it marked the beginning of most renewal chapters and the involvement of the entire membership in the preparation.

Even though rates of entry decreased in the latter 1960's, there are a few orders that continued to recruit significant numbers of women as late as 1969 and 1970. Is it possible to characterize these orders, especially in terms of the degree to which the orders had effected change? The issue of how structural change relates to rates of entry is interesting especially in the light of Pope Pius XII's remarks to the superiors general gathered in Rome for the international congress described in the opening of this book. The pope urged that the causes for the decline in vocations and the lack of perseverance of postulants and novices be carefully studied and conditions remedied so that more young women would desire to join convents. In his closing address he said, "Make sure nothing in your customs, your manner of life, or your ascetical practices raises a barrier or causes loss of vocation. We have in mind certain usages, which were no doubt suited to the times and surroundings in which they were instituted, but are out of place today, so that even a good girl with courage would find them an obstacle in her vocation."[1]

In this study, analysis was done of the relationship between structural change in an order and rates of women entering the order. Hypothesis I maintained that the rate and types of changes being initiated are related to the decreasing number of new members and that those orders most change oriented would be drawing the fewest numbers of recruits, while the more conservative orders would continue to recruit large numbers of women. When rate of entry for all eleven years is correlated with degree of structural change in the order, the resulting Pearson's r coefficient is not significant. Thus, for the eleven-year span the hypothesis that the more conservative orders are drawing the largest numbers of new members is not supported. However, the nine orders that have an entry rate of 10% or higher are orders that have low change scores. Since these orders are few in number, they do not show up as statistically significant in the overall analysis. However, this observation suggests that it is important to pursue further the analysis of the relationship between change and entry rates.

One possibility is that a relationship between rate of entry and degree of change could exist for individual years within the eleven-year period but that the relationship is lost in a general analysis of all the years. Correlation of change and entry rate for each year shows a statistically significant relationship for the two years 1964 and 1970. In 1964 there was a slight positive relationship between degree of change and rate of entry, that is, the more an order was beginning to effect change, the more new members it was drawing. Even though the relationship is statistically significant, the degree of relationship is very slight indeed, a Pearson's r coefficient of .18. By 1964 no order had effected much change, so that it is impossible to conclude much from this relationship. In 1970, however, a stronger relationship exists (Pearson's r of $-.32$), significant at the .01 level, and it is a negative relationship, that is, the more structural change an order has effected, the lower the rate of entry. In effect, then, the pattern reversed itself between 1964 and 1970 such that change was positively related to entries in 1964 and negatively so in 1970.

In order to look more closely at the relationship between change and entry rates, orders were disaggregated on the basis of degree of change, and those orders most change oriented (change score of 4) were compared with those orders least change oriented (change score of 0). For each of the years 1960, 1964, 1967, and 1970, the change orders had higher entry rates than the nonchange orders. However, an interesting pattern emerges. In 1960, 53% of the change orders had an entry rate of 10% or higher compared with 16% of the nonchange group. In 1964, comparable figures were 33% for change orders and only 13% for nonchange orders. By 1967, however, the difference in percentages for the two groups diminished significantly, with 26% of the change orders having a rate of 10% or higher compared with 23% of the nonchange orders. The same pattern exists for 1970, when four change orders or 25% had entrance rates of 10% or higher compared with 21% for the nonchange orders. Between 1960 and 1970, therefore, there was a 28 percentage point drop in entrance rates for the change orders compared with only a 5 point drop for nonchange orders.

In effect, then, in the early part of the decade, change and modernization in religious orders seemed to attract women to join the group, but by the end of the decade fewer were entering orders in general and the orders that had modernized least were experiencing less drastic drops in entries than others that had changed most. This means, in effect, that the pressure to update and modernize may have severe consequences upon the survival of the order. Hypothesis I, then, is verified to the extent that between 1960 and 1970 a larger proportion of change orders experienced more drastic decreases in number entering than did the nonchange orders.

Membership Losses, 1960–1970

While canon law in the church has, since its inception, provided for dispensations from religious vows and the return to a lay state, until the 1970's the provision was rarely used. The granting of a dispensation is reserved to a special church tribunal, the Sacred Congregation for Religious, which considers applications and passes judgment on whether the reasons stated by the applicant make it impossible for her to be faithful to her vows. Historically, few applications were received each year, and the phenomenon of a nun with permanent vows leaving her order was rare. However, beginning in the early 1960's the number of members already permanently professed who were leaving increased steadily. This outflux of members and, concomitantly, the decreasing numbers of new members during the 1960's had an effect on the numbers of religious women in the United States.

There are three formal mechanisms which an individual can utilize to disaffiliate herself, either permanently or temporarily, from her order. A dispensation, also known technically as an "indult of secularization," is the permission granted to a nun by the church to live permanently "in the world" without any further connection with the institute in which she made vows. Once the dispensation is granted by the Sacred Congregation for Religious in Rome, the individual no longer has rights or obligations vis-à-vis the institute. All legal and moral bonds are terminated between the person and the order in which she has been a member.

Both a leave of absence and an exclaustration are temporary withdrawals from the order and carry with them a time limit. An exclaustration, according to canon law, is the permission by which a nun is allowed to remain temporarily outside the convent and to be exempt for a time from the authority of the superiors of the order. Under exclaustration, a nun remains bound by her vows; however, she may not wear the religious habit and she forfeits both the right to run for office in the order and the right to vote. Exclaustrations were originally given on the basis of either health or apostolic work that the person wanted to do for a limited time. However, in recent years they have been granted more freely and for a diversity of reasons, including the opportunity to reevaluate one's vocation and desire to remain in the order.

The granting of an exclaustration was an unusual event prior to the 1960's. However, as more and more requests were made to the Sacred Congregation for exclaustrations, the Sacred Congregation issued a document in 1966 to every major superior giving them the power to grant "leaves of absence" to members who wanted permission to live outside the order for a time. A "leave of absence" is not as radical a break with the order as an exclaustration since the member on leave maintains the right to hold office and vote and remains subject to her superiors in the order. However, a member on leave is freed from many communal obligations, especially the requirement to live with other members of the order.

While slight distinctions do exist between a leave of absence and an exclaustration, which one is applied for by the individual is frequently left to the policy or practice of the order rather than to the request of the member. Some orders prefer their members to apply to the Sacred Congregation for an exclaustration while others are willing to grant leaves of absence themselves.

The majority of individuals who request a leave of absence or an exclaustration subsequently apply for a dispensation. In fact, then, a temporary withdrawal is usually a preliminary step to complete severing of ties and serves, in many cases, as a stage of socialization back into the major society.

The following table shows the dramatic increase in the numbers of

Table 4. *Number of permanent members leaving by year*

N = 287

Year	No. receiving permanent or temporary withdrawals	Numerical change	Percentage change
1960	220		
1961	261	+41	+19%
1962	309	+48	+18%
1963	303	−6	−2%
1964	468	+165	+54%
1965	532	+64	+14%
1966	820	+288	+54%
1967	1,401	+581	+71%
1968	1,681	+280	+20%
1969	2,439	+758	+45%
1970	2,815	+376	+15%
Total	11,249		

nuns who left during the 1960's. No distinction is made in this table between temporary and permanent withdrawals. Since the same individual could request a temporary leave one year and then request permanent severance a following year, the numbers must be interpreted as number of *requests* rather than number of individuals leaving. Table 5 will differentiate temporary and permanent severance. In 1960, 220 individuals with permanent vows in the 287 orders included in the study requested some type of permanent dispensation or temporary leave of absence from their vows. By 1970 the number rose to 2,815, almost thirteen times as many. Between 1960 and 1970 there was a yearly increase in the number seeking permission to leave, with the exception of a very slight decrease (6 people) between 1962 and 1963. The largest increment in the number receiving dispensations and leaves occurred in 1969, and 758 more people left than in 1968. The second largest numerical increase was in 1967, when 581 more requests were granted than in the previous year.

One reason for the unusually large increases in 1966–1967 and 1968–1969 was the timing of events in the renewal movement, especially the occurrence of renewal chapters in religious orders. In June, 1966, *Motu Proprio* was issued by Pope Paul VI. This was the document that initiated the implementation of change in religious orders.

By the end of 1967 the document had been studied by most nuns, either directly or through workshops, and it was possible to determine to some extent the pace and degree of change that would be effected in various orders. Also, by 1967 renewal and reform had become daily conversation in most convents, and nuns began questioning aspects of their lives that previously went unquestioned. By 1967 the possibility and procedure of obtaining leaves of absence and dispensations began to become common knowledge, and most nuns knew personally someone who had left.

During 1968 the majority of religious orders held their special renewal chapters mandated by Pope Paul in his implementation document. Some orders convoked a first session in the summer of 1967, but summer, 1968, marked the close of most chapters and the implementation of changes that had been studied and voted upon by the chapter delegates. By 1969 members in most orders knew the direction that renewal would take in their order and were able to use this knowledge to make a decision regarding their own life.

In the initial survey to religious orders, no attempt was made to distinguish the ways in which individuals requested freedom from their vows and obligations to the institutes in which they were members. In order to be as nonthreatening as possible and to obtain a general picture of the magnitude of numbers leaving, the question on "leavers" was very general. Encouraged by the good response to the first questionnaire, the second one included more detailed and refined questions on numbers of individuals withdrawing from the order. Most importantly, the second set of data differentiates permanent and temporary withdrawals. Because these data are more precise, permanent dispensations will be used most frequently throughout this book to analyze rates of leaving and organizational relationships. The use of this refined data diminishes the number of orders used in the analysis to 184. However, as indicated in Appendix 3, there is no significant bias in this sample so that it is representative of religious orders in the United States during the period being considered.

Table 5 indicates the number of dispensations and temporary leaves that were granted each year between 1960 and 1970. Not only the number of dispensations increased steadily in the sixties but also the number of temporary leaves. By 1968 almost two-thirds as many requested temporary leaves as the number asking for dispensations. When, in some of our subsequent analysis, therefore, the number of dispensations is used as a measure of leaving, the measure is conservative when considering those who are experiencing alienation or disaffiliation with their order.

Table 5. *Number of members dispensed, exclaustrated, and on leave by year*

N = 184

Year	No. dispensed	Percentage change	No. exclaustrated	Percentage change	No. on leave	Percentage change
1960	141		20		0	
1961	146	+4%	4	−80%	3	+300%
1962	113	−23%	6	+50%	12	+300%
1963	141	+25%	16	+167%	21	+75%
1964	224	+59%	25	+56%	22	+5%
1965	321	+43%	28	+12%	16	−27%
1966	367	+14%	48	+71%	34	+113%
1967	609	+66%	119	+148%	69	+103%
1968	683	+12%	263	+128%	192	+33%
1969	984	+44%	334	+27%	284	+48%
1970	1,068	+9%	359	+7%	329	+16%
Total	4,797		1,222		982	

After 1966 the number of temporary leaves that were granted increased significantly each year and probably reduced the number of dispensations requested in any one year. However, taking only the number dispensed as a measure of the number of individuals leaving each year, there is still significant increase yearly after 1965. Table 5 shows the numerical increase in those leaving each year. Again, the two largest increments occurred in 1967 and 1969. Whether the 1970 increase of 84 people is part of the two-year pattern between 1966 and 1969, that is, a large increment in numbers leaving every other year, or whether it marks a slowdown of the trend to be continued during the 1970's awaits further data on what happened in the years since 1970. It is impossible, on the basis of data from the 1960's, to make any predictions as to what is happening to religious orders in the 1970's regarding the maintenance of members, due primarily to the unique series of events in the church related to the Vatican Council in the early 1960's.

It is obvious from the previous data that the number of religious women seeking both temporary and final dispensations from their commitment to the religious order in which they made a life vow has increased steadily during the decade of the sixties and throughout the first year of the seventies. The exodus, however, did not occur randomly throughout American orders; rather, variations existed among orders in the number and rates of individuals that were leaving. The mean number that left per order is 29.9. However, the range in numbers leaving is from 0 to 218 with a median of 21.8. There is sig-

Table 6. *Rate of dispensations by order, 1960–1970*

N = 184

Rate of dispensations	No. of orders	% of orders that responded
0	16	13
1–3	11	9
4–6	28	23
7–9	30	24
10–12	17	14
13–15	7	5
16–19	5	4
20–29	6	5
30–40	4	3
No data	60	—
Total	184	100

Mean: 8.8
Median: 6.8

nificant variation, therefore, among orders in the number who left during the 1960's to allow meaningful comparisons on various organizational variables.

Table 6 translates numbers leaving into rates of leaving, that is, the number of people leaving the order proportionate to the total size of membership. Rates of leaving were based upon the number who obtained permanent dispensations. Considering rates of leaving, the mean rate for all 184 orders was 8.8% with a median rate of 6.8%. Rates of leaving range from 0 to 40% with a majority of orders falling in the lower categories. Forty-seven percent of the orders experienced a 4–9% loss. Another 22% had between 0–3% leaving, for a combined total of 69% of the orders having less than 10% of their membership leaving. Ten orders or 8% experienced over a 20% loss in the eleven-year period.

It is obvious from table 6 that the phenomenon of membership losses did not occur at the same rate in all orders. It therefore becomes important to consider the question of whether any organizational differences, especially degree of change effected in the order, are related to rates of leaving.

Organizational Change and Rates of Leaving

A central hypothesis of the present study is that the orders that have effected more structural change in the direction of greater decentralization and personal freedom have lost more members than orders not having experienced such radical changes. Calculating a correlation coefficient for the relationship between degree of change and rate of leaving for all 184 orders produces a result that is not statistically significant at the .05 level ($r = .09$). In other words, there is no systematic relationship between the two variables such that one could predict the rate at which members left the order on the basis of the degree of change in the order.

Hypothesis II, therefore, which predicted that orders with greater structural change would have experienced higher rates of membership withdrawals, is not supported. The same lack of relationship existed when comparing change scores and rates of entrance. However, a significant relationship did exist when only the most liberal orders, that is, those with a score of 4 on the change index, were compared with the most conservative, namely, orders having a score of 0. For these orders with extreme scores, those with high change scores experienced more drastic declines in the number of new recruits than did the orders with low change scores. Does a similar pattern exist between change and rates of leaving?

Considering only those orders with the highest and lowest change scores, change orders have experienced proportionately higher rates of leaving. Of the orders with a score of four, 54% lost 10% or more of their membership during the 1960's compared with 29% of the orders scoring 0 on the change index. Testing these two proportions statistically by a difference in proportions test shows that the difference is statistically significant at the .05 level. For the extreme cases, therefore, that is, those orders that effected the most change during the 1960's and those that effected least, there is a relationship between change and leaving such that the change orders lost more members and at the same time gained fewer new members than the nonchange orders. For the 86 orders with change scores between the two extremes, no relationship exists between change and rates of leaving.

In an attempt to understand the meaning of the previous finding, it is important to recall the meaning of the change index, that is, the empirical items that went into its construction. The 25 conservative orders are characterized by prescriptions of uniform dress, uniform prayer and ritual regulations, assignment to both jobs and living situation by central authority with no individual choice allowed, and finally, financial arrangements such that the individual has no control over money matters. In summary, the orders scoring 0 on the index have effected no substantial change in the above five structural areas, despite the forces pushing toward change both officially in church documents and within the general milieu of renewal in religious orders.

The 11 orders that scored at the opposite extreme, that is, the most liberal orders, have radically restructured in the five areas so that in all cases some degree of individual choice is allowed. The orders scoring between the two extremes have effected change in some of the five structural areas but not in others.

For orders that have initiated radical change in basic areas of traditional religious life, therefore, those changes are associated with greater rates of leaving from the community and returning to a secular life. Why this pattern exists cannot be explained on the basis of organizational variables but rather must be understood in terms of why women in liberal orders chose to sever their membership. As interview data in chapter five will show, many of the women who left liberal orders felt the order no longer afforded them sufficient reason and meaning for belonging since most of the activities in which they were engaged in the renewed order were possible outside its boundaries. What occurred in many orders that initiated far-reaching changes after Vatican II was that structural change outpaced ideological or goal-oriented change such that renewed structures were based on greater individual freedom and responsibility without a concomitant emphasis upon the value of corporate membership. Women who previously did not experience individual choice and decision making were initially enthusiastic and committed to the notions of personal responsibility and initiative. Many of them were even influential in helping to bring about these changes. However, after a time of individual freedom, the question raised by many of them was whether belonging to the order provided unique resources or rewards not available outside the group. Many women who left change-oriented groups felt they could achieve the same goals in a secular life and not be restricted by such institutionalized demands as celibacy.

The orders that did not make allowances for individual choice in basic structural areas never afforded members the new experience of personal decision making. Emphasis was still upon group uniformity and a strong sense of obedience and sharing in a common life that was deeply rooted in past tradition and history. In these orders, fewer women opted to leave the group.

This basic finding that very liberal orders lost more members than very conservative orders supports the conclusions of a number of studies on utopian communities that demonstrate the necessity of clearly defined group goals and a sense of the value of individual sacrifice in order to achieve those goals. Rosabeth Kanter, in her analysis of nineteenth century utopias, isolates three types of commitment mechanisms that differentiated successful (that is, long-lived) groups from unsuccessful ones: (1) *sacrifice*, that is, the process of members being asked to give up something as a price of membership; (2) *investment*, the process of providing the individual with a stake in the fate of the community; and (3) *renunciation*, relinquishing of relationships that are potentially disruptive to group cohesion.[2] Each mechanism involves individual costs sacrificed for the superordinate goals of the group. Utopias began to disintegrate and dissolve when individual members no longer saw sufficient value in group goals to renounce personal gratifications.

Oneida disintegrated when internal dissension arose over the degree of personal sacrifice required for the unity and centralization of the community. As more young people were educated in the secular society they refused to renounce individual choice and personal wants for the goals of the group.[3]

Gillian Lindt Gollin dates the transformation of the Moravian Brethren from a religious community to a modern industrial society from the time when economic enterprises were placed in the hands of individuals rather than guided and directed by centralized group authorities. The process of greater individualization and personal decision making led to a deemphasis upon group values and finally to a total transformation of group identity.[4] These studies, as well as others on utopian groups, point out the necessity in this type of social organization of clearly defined group goals, group solidarity, and sacrifice of individual goals for those explicitly maintained by the group.

The data on religious orders presented in this chapter support this fact of utopian groups. Those orders that deemphasized group uniformity suffered greater membership losses than those orders that maintained centralized control in basic decision areas. Given the fact that the very liberal orders experienced the greatest decline in number of members entering the order as well as increase in numbers leaving, it is possible that orders experiencing radical structural change may not survive the present crisis of change. In those orders that are effecting moderate change but maintaining some degree of centralization and uniformity, the pattern of members leaving is not as striking as in either of the extreme cases.

Because of the variation that exists within religious orders in terms of the kinds of changes that have been introduced since Vatican II and the varying rates of leaving from different orders, it is important to discover whether any organizational variables are predictive of either change or leaving within religious orders. Is the degree of structural change in an order simply a random or unique phenomenon such that patterns among orders are nonexistent, or do patterns emerge when organizational characteristics are isolated? The same question arises when considering rates of departures. On the basis of the data already presented in this chapter it is possible to predict patterns in rates of leaving for the most liberal and conservative orders. Are any other organizational variables predictive of varying rates of leaving?

Religious Variables, Change, and Membership Losses

Religious orders differ from profit-making business organizations or from secular service organizations precisely in the area of their "religiousness." Within orders there are variations in how religious spirit and practice are lived out. It is important, therefore, to consider the impact of religious differences upon the degree to which the order responded to Vatican II's call for change and renewal and also the numbers of women who opted out of the order in the decade of renewal.

The historical origin of all religious orders was the desire of holy men in the church, many of them religious charismatics, to found a group of women who would dedicate their entire lives, giving up a family and all that entails, to minister as "spiritual mother" to the needs of people. The motivation behind such radical giving was to witness to Jesus and his teachings. Therefore, most constitutions propose a twofold goal for the order: (1) the glory of God and sanctification of the members through (2) apostolic service to the needs in the church.

While orders share these broad goals, founders of orders inculcated different "spirits" and gave stress to different virtues. This is reflected in the constitutions which the founder selected for his group and the "fundamental virtues" which are stressed in the formal constitution of an order.

In the document on renewal in religious life promulgated by the council fathers and in *Motu Proprio*, issued later by Pope Paul, religious orders were encouraged to return to the two primary inspirations of the order: (1) the gospels and (2) the spirit and life of the founder. The process of renewal in religious orders, therefore, accentuated differences in spirit, religious motivations, and religious virtues that are to characterize members of the institute. Within the last decade a growing number of theologians and writers of various sorts are specializing in the area of "discernment of the spirit in the order," and it is becoming popular to hire such consultants to assist chapters in rediscovering the uniquenesses given by the founder to the order.

Since reflection upon the spirit of an order, formalized in its constitution, the fundamental virtues stressed by the founder, and specific apostolic thrusts have become conscious considerations by chapters in the process of renewal, it is possible that such ideologies and motivational thrusts directed chapter delegates in their decisions regarding changes in the order. This can be tested empirically in the present study to the extent that orders who responded to the survey listed the "Great Rule" upon which their constitutions were based, the fundamental virtues which have been stressed in the order as a heritage from their founder, and the specific service tasks performed by the order.

Historically, there are four "Great Rules" or Declarations of Purpose and Ways of Living upon which religious orders were founded: those of St. Augustine, St. Benedict, St. Francis of Assisi, and St. Ignatius of Loyola. A founder usually based the constitutions for his new community on one of these "Great Rules," and in recent centuries in the church, this became a requirement for the approval of a new order.

While each of the rules stressed love of God, personal sanctity, and service of one's neighbor, each one put emphasis upon different means. The Rule of St. Augustine is the oldest of the rules. While it is debatable whether it was written by Augustine himself, the contents of the rule reflect some of his basic teachings, primarily the value of the common life and the need for abstinence and authority that are essential for people living together for religious purposes. Because of its stress upon community life and brotherhood, over 150 orders follow that rule today.

St. Benedict originally drew up his rule for monks. It was later adapted for the use of women. Until the seventh century, most nuns followed rules given to them by their local bishops, who devised them in eclectic fashion from existing rules. The Rule of St. Benedict gradually supplanted other rules and became the standard guide for most convents until the twelfth century. It is characterized by its conceptualization of a religious order as a family whose head is the superior who is responsible for the temporal and spiritual welfare of the community. While the superior is the center of unity for the group, she consults the entire community when important matters are involved. The family life envisioned by Benedict is the fruit of a spiritual orientation which comes from an appreciation of the liturgy. Hence, his great stress upon liturgical celebrations.

The rule that St. Francis of Assisi left his followers is summarized in his wanting them to live simply as Jesus lived on earth. This finds its fullest manifestation in what Francis called poverty, a practical detachment from self and from creatures. His followers were to use creatures but never possess them as their own. A characteristic of Franciscans, therefore, was love for all of creation, but a type of love that engendered respect and care without possession. Followers of Francis were to own nothing personally because such ownership might lead to attachment. Instead, they were to depend on the good will and generosity of people to provide them the necessities of life.

The Rule of St. Ignatius is unique in its stress on absolute obedience to the church and the apostolic commitment of members to go wherever the pope sent them and to the goal of being soldiers of Christ in the midst of the world. Up until the time of Ignatius, religious life was basically monastic. Nuns and monks withdrew from the world in order to dedicate themselves to prayer and fasting. Ignatius founded a group of men who were to go among the people as ''soldiers of Christ'' in order to bring Christ to the world. Since the pope was Christ's visible representative in the world, the followers of Ignatius, known as Jesuits, were to vow absolute obedience to him.

Fifty-six percent of the orders studied had constitutions based upon the Rule of St. Augustine. This is due primarily to the fact that his rule stresses the common life and is compatible and supportive to the active purposes for which most orders were founded. The 20% based on the Rule of St. Francis and the 12% based on St. Benedict's rule are primarily those Franciscan and Benedictine orders founded by each of the two saints of the church. Seven percent follow the Rule of St. Ignatius and the remaining 5% of the orders are based on various minor rules approved by the church.

When orders are compared on the basis of which of the rules they follow, no significant relationship exists between the rule and rates at which orders lost members during the 1960's. The same lack of relationship exists for the rule of the order and degree of change.

In addition to differences among orders in the ''Great Rule'' upon which they were founded, each order emphasizes different ''fundamental virtues'' which are to characterize members in that order. Usually, these fundamental virtues were stressed by the founder as hallmarks or signs of the members in that order. Among religious women, there is a tacit understanding and recognition of the virtues which characterize women in different orders. For example, Dominicans stress truth and learning, Benedictines emphasize liturgy and prayer, and Franciscans are simple and poor. Do such differences in characteristic virtues relate to how an order changes or how many women exit from the order?

Analysis relating fundamental virtues which are to characterize members of the order and both degree of change effected and rate at which members left the order also revealed no significant differences among orders. The greatest proportion of the orders that responded listed charity as their primary fundamental virtue, 26%, followed by 20% listing simplicity, and 17% mentioning truth. The remaining 37% varied in the virtue they mentioned as their primary practice. There is enough variation, therefore, for any real differences among orders to show up when virtues of an order are compared with varying rates of leaving. The fact that no statistical difference results indicates that the virtue characteristic of members of an order is not related to whether people are leaving the order or not. The same lack of relationship holds true for the relationship of primary virtue to degree of change. Practicing any particular virtue does not make an order more or less apt to have a given degree of structural change.

Another dimension of religious orders that must be taken into account in attempting to explain variations in numbers leaving is the type of apostolic work to which the order has traditionally been dedicated. Each founder of a religious order created the group to do a special work in the church. Teaching and hospital work in church-related institutions have been the two primary service occupations for religious women throughout their history in the United States. However, there are a few orders dedicated to other tasks, such as religious instructions outside of parochial schools, social work, running of orphanages and homes for the abandoned, retreat work, and service in the foreign missions. It is possible that the type of work of an order could affect the maintenance of membership commitment during periods of change. Particularly, the crises that Catholic schools are facing across the nation could well be creating anxieties and doubts in those orders whose membership is primarily prepared for that service.

Of the 161 orders that listed their primary apostolate, 126 were primarily dedicated to teaching in Catholic schools, 15 to working in Catholic hospitals, 14 to religious instruction in Catholic parishes, and the remaining 6 to other works. When rate dispensed is considered in relations to the primary work of an order, however, there is no significant relation between the two variables. Orders engaged in different works are losing members at about the same rates.

Looking at unique cases, however, it is interesting to note that the one order engaged principally in foreign mission work lost only 1.3%

of its membership during the eleven-year period, and the two orders doing social work lost less than 6%. These five instances are not sufficient to build a case for the fact that perhaps a more specific and limited apostolic thrust might lead to greater membership commitment; however, it is suggestive of the need to further analyze this variable in subsequent research, perhaps by conducting case studies comparing orders in limited apostolates outside of teaching with orders that define their goal in broad teaching terms or in the usual threefold categories which frequently are so broad they are meaningless, namely, education, health, and welfare work.

The above results indicate that type of religious practice or apostolic thrust in an order is not related to degree of change in the order nor to the rate of people leaving the order. Even though the council fathers instructed religious orders to renew and update in the light of the unique religious spirit given by their founder, such religious differences have no impact on either structural change in the order or exodus rates.

4. Education and the Exodus

In previous chapters, emphasis was placed upon the educational processes occurring within religious orders since the early 1950's, when Pope Pius XII instructed superiors general to educate their nuns consonant with other professional women. It was hypothesized that increased educational levels lead to greater change and also to increased numbers leaving. With the impact and success of the Sister Formation Movement during the late 1950's and early 1960's, educational levels within religious orders did in fact increase, especially in terms of higher degrees. Since few orders operated their own colleges and universities, women studying for master's degrees and doctorates were sent to institutions all over the country to study, many of them secular institutions. The Sister Formation Movement, therefore, resulted not only in increasing numbers of nuns being more highly educated but also provided them the experience of associating with seculars outside the cloister. For the first time in the history of religious orders, women left the convents to live and study with members not of the group. It was predicted that an unanticipated consequence of higher educational levels would be increases in rates of leaving due to more and more exposure to alternative life-styles. Concomitantly, the perceived cost of the personal renunciation required in religious life would increase. In this chapter this hypothesis will be empirically tested by comparing educational levels and rates of leaving within religious orders.

There is another interpretation, however, that must be considered in predicting a positive association between level of education and rate of leaving among nuns, namely, the job opportunity structure confronted by educated and less-educated women. As nuns became better educated, job opportunities expanded for them, not only within their own orders but also in society outside the cloister. Interview data suggest that some nuns without professional degrees were deterred from leaving by the prospect of not finding a desirable job. While nuns were allowed in the old system to teach and nurse without appropriate degrees, they realized that secular institutions will normally not make such allowances. As nuns obtained professional training their advantage in the job market increased, thereby reducing some of the anxiety and tension associated with leaving convent life. A positive relationship between education and leaving could, therefore, simply be the result of greater job opportunities.

Each of the above interpretations will be tested by comparing data on leaving for both educated and less-educated nuns. If only the educated are leaving, either interpretation would be feasible. However, if both groups are leaving, the opportunity structure argument would not be sufficient explanation for the relationship.

Education and Rates of Leaving

By 1971, when the survey was conducted, most religious orders had few members who did not have college degrees, so that to use college degree as an indicator of educational level would have provided little discrimination among orders. On the other extreme of the education continuum, most orders had some members who had acquired doctoral degrees. However, in most orders this number of highly educated women constituted a very small proportion of the membership. To have utilized rate of doctorates in the order as a measure of education would also have provided little discrimination among orders.

In the case of master's degrees, a broader range existed among orders in the proportion of women with M.A. degrees. As table 7 indicates, the median rate of education for all orders was 19.5, that is, half the orders had more women than that with master's degrees and half had fewer women with M.A.'s. Fifteen percent of the orders had fewer than 10% of their membership with M.A. degrees. On the other hand, 27 orders or 26% had over 30% with master's. In general, then, a large number of religious orders (56%) had a rate of 20% or higher of members with master's degrees.

It is also the case that most master's degrees had to be obtained outside the order at accredited institutions of higher learning. The factor of association with seculars, therefore, characterizes women with M.A.'s as well as with Ph.D.'s although the length of time required to obtain the degree necessarily differed.

Educational level, therefore, is measured empirically by the number of individuals in an order with a master's degree in 1971 plus those who had left between 1960–1970 with a master's degree, divided by the size of the order. One hundred and three of the 184 orders reported complete data on number of M.A.'s in the order, number M.A.'s leaving, and size of order, so that for these 103 orders it is possible to

Table 7. *Rate of master's degrees within orders*

N = 184

Rate M.A.	No. of orders	% of orders
0	0	0.0
1–4	4	3.9
5–9	11	10.7
10–14	14	13.6
15–19	16	15.5
20–24	16	15.5
25–29	15	14.6
30–39	17	16.5
40–49	7	6.7
50+	3	3.0
No data	81	—
Total	184	100.0

Mean: 19.4
Median: 19.5

calculate educational level of the order. The present chapter, therefore, bases analysis on these 103 orders. (See Appendix 3 for representativeness of sample.)

Hypothesis III predicted that the higher the level of education in an order, the higher the rate of leaving. When orders are compared by rate of education and rate of leaving, Pearson's $r = .31$, significant at the .001 level. Orders with higher educational levels had higher rates of women leaving. Empirical evidence, therefore, supports the hypothesis that increased educational levels in religious orders lead to increased numbers of women opting to give up their membership and return to secular life.

There are several possible processes that could be operating to explain the above finding and that must be taken into consideration in attempting to explain the positive relationship. First, I suggested earlier that it was an educated audience that heard and responded to Vatican II's call for renewal and change. Is it the case that high educational levels in religious orders are associated with structural change such that women who received higher degrees outside the order returned to their orders, initiated changes in the direction of greater personalism and individual responsibility in the order, and then decided there was insufficient reason for remaining in the order? If this is the case, then change would function as an intervening variable. Higher educational levels would lead to greater structural change, which in turn would effect higher rates of women leaving the order.

A second process or factor that must be considered is whether those women who have received master's degrees are, in fact, those who are leaving. The assumption, up to this point in the study, is that increased contact with outsiders on the part of those women studying outside the cloister led to greater awareness of alternative life-styles and influenced these women to reevaluate their choice of religious life in the light of alternatives. However, it is possible that women who received master's degrees returned to their orders and created a milieu or organizational climate that encouraged the rethinking of religious commitment not only on their part but for all members in the order, including those who did not have the opportunity of studying outside the group. In the latter case, increasing educational levels could be associated with increasing rates of leaving but would not necessarily mean that those women with master's degrees were the ones opting to leave the order. Put more succinctly, is the relationship between education and leaving an individual phenomenon, that is, occurring within the same individuals, or is it an organizational, contextual variable that refers to the creation of a climate by educated members such that leaving occurs on the part of increasing numbers of women, not necessarily those who themselves received the education?

First, consideration is given to the possibility that rate of education is associated with structural change such that increased education leads to greater change, which in turn is associated with women leaving. When degree of structural change is related to educational level, $r = .20$, significant at the .01 level. Those orders with high educational levels have experienced the greatest structural change. When orders are grouped into those with a low rate of education (less than 20% of members with M.A.'s) and orders with a high education rate (20% or more members with M.A.'s), the less-educated orders have a median change score of 1.2 compared with 2.4 for educated orders. In effect, therefore, those orders with a higher proportion of educated women are more liberal structurally than less highly educated orders. This finding indicates that education does result in modernization.

Given the fact that education is associated with both greater structural changes and higher rates of leaving, it is important to consider the second process that could be operating to explain the relationship be-

Table 8. *Rate of leaving for women with M.A.*
degrees and without M.A. degrees
for all orders

N = 103

Rate of leaving	With M.A.	Without M.A.
Mean	12.2	7.1
Median	9.1	5.8
S.D.	13.2	7.9

tween educational level and rate of leaving, namely, whether it is the educated women themselves who are leaving. In other words, are those individuals with higher degrees the ones who are leaving religious orders or are the educated women creating an organizational climate in which all members, educated and uneducated alike, are questioning their original commitment? Table 8 shows that, for all orders, more women with M.A. degrees have left than women without master's degrees. The median rate of leaving for women with M.A.'s is 9.1 compared with 5.8 for women without M.A. degrees. Therefore, it is predominantly the educated women who are exiting. However, it is interesting that the difference in medians between the two groups is only 3.3 and that the rate for nondegreed women is as high as it is. The original prediction in the present study was that many more educated women were leaving because of their exposure outside the cloister.

The question that arises at this point is whether educational level in the order influences what happens to educated women when they return to their orders. Do educated women tend to stay in educated orders where there are others with similar experiences and backgrounds? Do they, on the other hand, tend to leave in greater proportions from less-educated orders where they would be a minority? In order to test these possibilities, orders were disaggregated on the basis of educational levels, that is, orders in which 20% or more members had a master's degree compared with orders in which less than 20% had a master's degree. When differences in rates of degreed and nondegreed women leaving educated and uneducated orders are compared (see table 9, column differences), there is a greater difference (4.4 points in medians) in the uneducated orders than in the educated orders (2.6 points difference in medians). The pattern, therefore, is that a greater proportion of degreed women than nondegreed women left uneducated orders

Table 9. *Median rate of women leaving with*
M.A. degrees and without M.A.
degrees by educational level of
order

Median rate of leaving	Educational level of order	
	Low* (N = 47)	High** (N = 56)
Women with M.A.	9.9	8.6
Women without M.A.	5.5	6.0

*Less than 20% of membership with M.A. degrees.
**20% or more with M.A. degrees.

than is true for educated orders. However, analysis of women with
M.A.'s and women without M.A.'s who left each group shows little
difference between educated and uneducated orders (row differences).
The median rate of leaving for educated women in educated orders is
8.6 compared with 9.9 for uneducated orders, a difference of only 1.3
points. For women without master's degrees, the median rates are 6.0
for educated orders and 5.5 for uneducated orders, an even smaller
difference in medians. The evidence, up to this point, indicates that
level of education in orders does not make a significant difference in
rates at which educated and uneducated women leave religious orders.

The fact that more educated than less-educated women are leaving
suggests that job opportunity might be operative in the process. However, such an interpretation would not explain why significant numbers
of uneducated women are also leaving. The fact that the difference in
rates for the two groups is relatively small suggests that a more plausi-
ble interpretation is that women who study in institutions outside their
own order are exposed to ideas and social contacts that can broaden
their perspective and provide new reference points for the individual.
However, such contacts have ramifications beyond those women directly exposed to them. As educated women return to their orders, they
bring with them perspectives that influence the entire organizational
climate, including ideas and evaluations of members who were not
themselves directly involved in the educational experience.

Size and Leaving Patterns

Throughout the literature on utopian groups, one organizational variable that emerges repeatedly as a major determinant of changes in group structure and group cohesiveness is that of size of the membership. Utopian communities are usually small enough to permit a high degree of membership solidarity and a sense of group belongingness. As Kanter points out, dilemmas arise for utopian groups as they begin to grow numerically and attempt to perpetuate an ideology and lifestyle beyond the original generation.[1]

Studies of various utopian groups show that one problem common among such groups as they increase in size is that of an expanding labor force with various skills and interests, not all of which can be fully utilized within the group itself. There exists a pattern within utopian groups of occupational diversification increasing with expanding size. Concomitantly, as occupations diversify, more and more members are allowed to seek employment outside the group. This innovation usually brings with it anxiety and fear on the part of group members that such outside contact will reduce group unity and a sense of cohesiveness.

Gollin, for example, shows that between 1727 and 1747 the Hutterite population increased from 300 to 800. At the same time, the number of different occupations of members rose from 24 to 73.[2] Available jobs within the community were soon filled, and in order to reduce the unemployment rate, members were allowed to seek employment outside the community. However, there was fear within the group that daily contact with outsiders would interfere with the founder's plan for a closely knit and self-sufficient community. Later, outside employment was forbidden for fear of its threatening group unity. Instead, restrictions of immigration to the community were instigated so that population size would not outstrip job opportunity.

Similarly, Spiro, in his study of an Israeli kibbutz, describes the fact that as size of membership increased, more individuals were given freedom to seek jobs in the outside world since the group could not absorb all of the specialties and skills of an expanding population. Therefore, since 1950 members are employed in various occupations outside the kibbutz, such as the Israeli Aircraft Industry, commercial firms, and research organizations. In order to prepare for specialized professions, more kibbutz members have been allowed to pursue advanced study outside kibbutz educational institutions. However, there is the ever-present fear among many kibbutz members that solidarity will never be strong as long as members are not engaged in intrakibbutz occupations.[3]

The close relationship between education and occupational preparedness means that as more members in utopian groups move into specialized professions both within and outside their group, it becomes more and more necessary to be professionally trained. As occupational diversity occurs, diversity in the educational training of members simultaneously occurs, so that with increased population size comes increased differentiation in educational levels also.

In the kibbutzim which Talmon studied, for example, the traditional pattern was for young people to be trained on the job by the experienced, older generation. However, as job opportunities became more scarce with an expanding second generation, more young people were allowed to go to secular universities and vocational schools for specializing training. Since positions demanding specialized training were limited within the kibbutzim, advanced training frequently led to occupations outside the group.[4]

Given the fact that organizational size has proven important in many utopian studies, especially in terms of structural change and occupational diversity, and given the fact that religious orders vary significantly in size of membership, it was predicted that size of the order would affect the relationship between educational level change and rates of leaving within religious orders. More specifically, on the basis of processes that have occurred in other utopian communities, it was hypothesized that small orders would have lower rates of education than large orders because job diversity and specialized occupational positions would be less common in small orders than in large ones. Also, in contrast to large orders, most small orders do not own or staff a college or university, so that obtaining advanced degrees is more expensive and more likely to expose members to new ideas and social contacts in that they must attend institutions not run by the order.

In order to test the effects of size upon change, rates of leaving, and educational levels, orders were grouped into two size categories, small and large orders, on the basis of number of members in the order. Small orders were defined in terms of fewer than 300 members, and large orders numbered 300 and over. The cutting point for defining small and large orders was determined by self-definition on the part of the orders themselves.[5]

First of all, considering educational level in both size groups, large orders have a slightly higher median rate of education than small orders: 20.0 for large orders compared with 18.6 for small orders. Previous data have shown that there exists a postive relationship between educational level in an order and rate of membership losses. This would lead to the prediction that small orders have a lower rate of leaving than large orders. This prediction is further warranted by the fact that small orders are also more conservative than large orders, a median change score of 1.4 for small orders compared with 2.2 for large orders. Since change and rate of leaving are positively related in the sample, the fact that small orders have a lower change score than large orders would lead one to expect that small orders would be losing fewer members.

However, when rate of leaving is compared for large and small orders, small orders, in fact, have a higher median rate of leaving than large orders: 7.3 compared with 5.9 for large orders. Therefore, small orders are losing more members despite a lower rate of education and a lower change score. The important issue, therefore, is what distinguishing characteristics of small orders might explain their higher exodus rates.

One reason for the discrepancy could be that small orders are losing more educated people than large orders because of lack of occupational opportunity within the order for members with specialized training. Medium-sized and large orders usually own and operate a greater variety of institutions, such as high schools, colleges, and hospitals, than small orders. Until orders recently allowed more and more of their members to work outside institutionally owned settings, the job possibilities that were open to highly trained women within religious orders were very meager. Since small orders are more conservative than large orders and allow less individual freedom in job choice, occupations outside institutions staffed by the order were frowned upon or not permitted at all as a general pattern. This could lead to frustration on the part of educated women and ultimately to their severing ties with the group.

Case study data also indicate that administrators and policy makers in religious orders tend to be the more educated members. However, there are limited administrative positions available in any given order. Usually small orders have fewer such positions than larger ones so that the number of educated women who can serve in these administrative capacities is small in proportion to the number who have higher degrees.

As table 10 indicates, a striking pattern results when rate of M.A.'s leaving is looked at for the two size groups. The median rate of leaving for women with master's degrees in small orders is 11.5 compared with 7.0 in large orders. While more women without master's degrees also left from small orders (median: 6.0) than from large orders (me-

Table 10. *Rate of women leaving with M.A. degrees
and without M.A. degrees by size of order*

| Rate of leaving | Size of order | | Total |
	Small (N = 50)	Large (N = 53)	
Women with M.A.			
Mean	16.0	8.6	12.2
Median	11.5	7.0	9.1
S.D.	16.5	7.6	13.2
Women without M.A.			
Mean	8.4	5.9	7.1
Median	6.0	5.8	5.8
S.D.	10.8	3.1	7.9

dian: 5.8), the difference in medians is significantly higher for women with master's degrees who left small orders. What is happening, therefore, is that a larger number of small orders are losing women who have been educated while large orders are managing to keep significantly more of their degreed people. If the reason for this finding is, in fact, lack of job opportunity within small orders, it means that, during the 1960's, increases in educational preparation outstripped job opportunity in small orders such that many women were educated with master's degrees but few job openings for highly educated women existed within corporate institutions. Here is another case of following an official mandate but not anticipating consequences of such action.

Durkheim suggested in *The Division of Labor in Society* that size (density) of a society is related to a more diversified division of labor, that is, to greater specialization, because there are a greater number of individuals with potential for carrying out various societal functions. In organic, industrial society the impetus is toward nonsegmental, mutually interdependent relationships which provide an individual the freedom to specialize according to his or her unique talents and propensities. Durkheim emphasized the fact that a certain level of social density or size of population is necessary for specialization to be possible.[6] A similar pattern exists within organizations to the extent that larger organizations have need for more diverse specialists and can better afford to maintain them than smaller ones.[7]

Within religious orders, the pattern is evident in the fact that larger orders have need for such specialized jobs as community recruiter, public relations and communications expert, researcher, archivist, continuing education coordinator, and director of hospital personnel. Small orders cannot afford to free someone full time for each of these positions nor would the demands of the membership be sufficient to justify full-time positions. What frequently happens in small orders is that one person serves in two or three administrative capacities. For example, the directress of novices may also be the community recruiter. Large orders, therefore, frequently offer greater diversity in occupational specialization than smaller orders. An individual, therefore, who is experiencing job frustration has alternatives open to her that might not be available to members of smaller orders. In addition, large orders are structurally more liberal than small orders and allow greater individual freedom in job choice. Therefore, women have more opportunity to decide where their educational skills might be best utilized, both within the order as well as in jobs outside the parochial structure.

The Sister Formation Movement was very effective in its goal of assuring better educational backgrounds for religious women in the United States. However, leaders of the movement failed to realize the complex interplay between education, occupational opportunity, and membership commitment. Data in the present chapter indicate that women who did acquire master's degrees left in greater proportions than women who did not acquire higher degrees. This pattern was especially the case in small orders, where fewer job opportunities exist for highly educated women. Regardless of the educational level in small orders, the median rate of leaving for women with M.A.'s is 11.5 (see table 11). In large educated orders a smaller proportion of educated women left (median: 6.0). In addition to more job opportunities in large orders, highly educated orders are more liberal in their policies regarding occupations outside the order's corporate institutional commitments. Therefore, greater job opportunity that exists within large orders plus more liberal policies regarding outside employment might well explain the fact that fewer educated women are leaving highly educated, large orders.

In the type of organic society that Durkheim described, diversity and specialization in occupations lead to greater solidarity as members become more and more dependent upon one another. The basis of solidarity shifts from mechanical, segmental relationships among members to one of interdependence.[8] In religious orders, however, occupational diversity has occurred without a concomitant shift in the bases of cohesion and group solidarity. Goals of religious orders still center on

Table 11. *Median rate of leaving for women with M.A. degrees and*
without M.A. degrees by educational level of order

Rate of leaving	Educational level of order			
	Small orders		Large orders	
	Low (N = 23)	High (N = 27)	Low (N = 23)	High (N = 30)
Women with M.A.	11.5	11.5	9.0	6.0
Women without M.A.	5.0	7.2	5.9	5.6

service within religious institutions, and bonds of solidarity have not
been redefined explicitly in terms of values that transcend specific
works of service. Therefore, as more and more women become involved occupationally outside the order, the question of what unites
members and makes the group meaningful and distinct becomes more
poignant. While the women involved in nonparochial service may see
religious value in their work, frequently it is the less-educated members who feel diversity as a threat to the future of the group. As long as
cohesion and unity continue to be defined in terms of specific types of
service, occupational diversity that includes service outside of parochial institutions will be viewed by some members as a threat to group
identity. As will be suggested in the last chapter, a solution to the
organizational dilemma might well lie in a succession of goals such
that solidarity will be rooted either in redefined service goals or in
values other than task goals.

5. Why the Exodus from Religious Orders?

Chapters three and four focused upon organizational factors evident in the increasing exodus from religious orders. By analyzing organizational survey data, it was possible to explicate trends and patterns that characterize varying rates of leaving from different orders. The question still remains: *Why* did people leave? Are the reasons women left similar regardless of the order from which they exited or do patterns exist for different orders? Why did other women in the same order stay? Are the patterns of staying or leaving related to change or the lack of it in the order? These are the central questions addressed by the interview part of the research design.

The first part of this chapter presents data on women who left three selected orders. The last part of the chapter discusses why other women stayed.

Chapter one discussed the process characteristic of structural change in religious orders and in addition the type of ideological and theological questions that were raised at each stage in the renewal process. Early renewal chapters were concerned with such issues as whether identifiable garb was essential to being a nun in the modern world; what poverty, celibacy, and obedience meant in post–Vatican II terms; and how religious life could become more relevant in the post–Vatican II church. A second level of questioning that followed in many orders after they had lived for a few years with more liberal structures included the issues of how American nuns could contribute to the civil rights movement and the betterment of conditions for the poor and what the vow of poverty had to do with the genuine economic poverty of a fourth of America's population. At this stage, those few religious orders that had moved beyond the first level of questioning concerned themselves with issues outside of their own internal affairs.

After struggling with these social and humanitarian questions, a few orders by 1971 had begun to ask whether religious orders any longer had a viable function and legitimating goal that made it worthwhile to belong. The orders that were daring to ask this basic question were those in which much structural change had occurred and most day-today decisions regarding job contracts, living situation, financial freedom, and dress were being made on a personal level. The questions before chapters at this stage in renewal were: What corporate goals or existential meaning do religious life and a given community in particular have that make belonging advantageous to the individual? Can religious orders achieve goals that are impossible or at least more difficult to achieve on an individual level or in secular groups in society? Groups that were asking these questions were not only facing peripheral structural changes but questioning their very reason for being.

Zablocki, when studying the Bruderhof,[1] and Hostetler, in his analysis of the Amish,[2] discovered that some of the most valuable insights into group processes came from those who had once been part of the group but had severed their membership for various reasons. Frequently, they found that reasons for leaving were related to events in the group and decisions made by the group. Since the ex-member was no longer emotionally identified with the group, he or she was able, in many cases, to be more objective about group norms than members. The case of the ex-member and the perspective he or she has on the group is a unique variation of the insider-outsider perspective that Merton discusses.[3] Having once been an insider, the ex-member has knowledge and experience of day-to-day life in the group. Being presently an outsider, the person can, in many instances, have emotional distance from the group. In addition to data on why ex-members left, therefore, interviews with ex-members also provided insight into the change process going on within the orders from which interviewees exited.

Reasons for Leaving

Because of the developmental and evolutionary processes that characterized the types of questions and issues considered by religious orders at various stages in the renewal process, it was hypothesized in chapter two that reasons for leaving would vary for members of different orders according to the degree of change that had been effected in their order and that there would be intragroup similarity among women who had left the same order. At the same time, it was hypothesized that greater variation would exist in reasons for leaving among women from different orders. It was also predicted that reasons for leaving would be more frequently related to change or the lack of it in the liberal and conservative orders and that the reasons women were leaving the moderate-change order would be more personally oriented.

The general hypothesis, therefore, is that the reasons women left are related to what was going on in their orders; however, the precise relationship between reasons for leaving and what was occurring in the order differs for ex-members in each group. For the liberal order, it was predicted, the freedom and personal decisions that were left to the individual would lead some women to question why they belonged at all and what the order had to offer that was not available in a lay life (Hypothesis V). For the conservative order, women would be impatient with the lack of change or the directions change was taking and would leave because they saw little hope for change in the near future (Hypothesis VI). In the moderate order, the gradual and well-planned change would lead some women to admit that they were not contented in the order no matter what happened organizationally and that now they felt free to leave and find a life-style where they might be happy (Hypothesis VII).

If these hypotheses are verified, it means, paradoxically, that regardless of the changes an order makes, it can expect to lose some of its members. If it does not change in a significant way, it faces the threat of people leaving because of lack of change. If it changes radically and rapidly, it jeopardizes the commitment of some members to the basic goals of religious life. If it takes a moderate-change position and effects slower and more systematically planned changes, more and more members in the process will begin to face their own motivations and personal states of well-being and question whether they are or have ever been truly committed to the religious life-style. In other words, it is possible that the phenomenon of increasing numbers of women leaving religious orders is an inevitable part of the change process going on within these groups and cannot be resolved by policy decisions on the part of the organization.

The research design to test these hypotheses, as described in detail in chapter two, consisted of the selection of three orders, each characterized by a different degree of structural change. One order had begun the change process early and was among the most liberal orders in the United States (Order A); one had, by 1971, effected little change, and there seemed to be few signs of change in the near future (Order C); the third order fell somewhere in the middle of a change continuum since it had experienced a moderate degree of change and was still in the process of change when the study was conducted (Order B). The design called for interviewing 20 women who had left each order during the years of renewal, 1965–1971. As stated in chapter two, because of limitations and difficulties in contacting some of the interviewees, only 19 women who had left each order were finally interviewed.

The method used to study the why's of leaving and staying in religious orders was reason analysis. For many years, consumer agencies and political groups have been asking people, "why," why they buy a certain product or why they vote a given way. Beginning in the 1930's such survey researchers as Paul Lazarsfeld and Arthur Kornhauser began developing approaches and methods to obtain better information and understanding of behavioral processes involved in the actions being surveyed.[4] What they developed was the technique that came to be known as reason analysis, a way to analyze how an individual's behavior is determined, not just statically but through a series of influences and decisions. Since that time reason analysis has been used to study various types of action: choosing an occupation (Lazarsfeld, 1931), getting married or divorced (Goode, 1956), joining a voluntary association (Sills, 1957), going to a psychoanalyst (Kadushin, 1958), and deciding to study in the United States (Ritterband, 1969).

The advantage of reason analysis over other forms of survey analysis is the method used for assessment of the cause of the action. Cross-sectional survey analysis counts the number of people who acted in a given way and describes characteristics of the actors compared with those of nonactors. In reason analysis, on the other hand, actors or, in some cases, nonactors, are asked why they did or did not do the given action and what influences led to their decision.

Charles Kadushin points out that a model of action, that is, a list of the basic elements in terms of which human action can be described, together with some notion of how action proceeds, is essential to the development of a scheme for analyzing why an action occurred. Such a scheme contains an organized list of all the factors that, for the specific action or decision being studied, can produce or inhibit an action.[5] All current models of action used in reason analysis emphasize the interplay between the subjective point of view and needs of an actor on the one hand, and the restraints, requirements, and stimulation of the environment on the other hand.

This model of action, emphasizing both individual decisions and organizational contexts, led in the present study to the development of an "accounting" scheme which included both personal factors and events occurring in the religious order of the interviewee. An "accounting scheme" is basically a list of factors that are involved in the why's of a decision. In regard to why individuals chose to leave a religious order, factors included in the interview guide were: dissatisfaction with the rate and direction of change in the order, positions of the Catholic Church hierarchy, specific incidents within the order, health, needs of family, loss of a sense of the meaning of religious life itself, professional limitations, desire to marry. A general question was asked as to why the individual decided to leave the order. This question was then followed by a series of questions relating to the factors included in the accounting scheme.

There was almost no hesitation or difficulty on the part of the interviewees in recalling why they left. In fact, this broad, general question elicited very definite and precise responses. This is due primarily to the fact that the decision to leave a religious order is a very conscious and well-thought-out decision which must be articulated not only to administrators in the orders but also to Roman authorities. The primary information required by both groups is why the person no longer feels she is able to live out her religious vows and wants to be relieved of them. One of the formal requisites, therefore, of exiting from a religious order is going through a very deliberate and conscious process of determining why one has decided to leave.

This requirement, however, of explicating reasons for requesting a dispensation from Rome does not necessarily mean that the reasons given to the Sacred Congregation are the actual motivating reasons for the person to leave the order. In fact, in the course of the interviews, it was discovered that various means exist to inform women requesting dispensations which reasons are acceptable to the Sacred Congregation and will merit a dispensation.

While I was aware of the discrepancies that existed between the formal reasons given to Rome for leaving and the genuine reasons that motivated the person to desire to leave the order, this did not pose a problem during the interviews, probably because the entire interview schedule emphasized personal dimensions of the decision process and deemphasized the formal process. However, I was aware of this discrepancy early in the interviewing and, on occasion, probed to make sure that the reasons being given during the interview were really the personal reasons of the individual and not the ones formalized to Rome.

In the accounting scheme that served as a general pattern for designing the interview schedule, reasons for leaving were divided into two basic categories: (1) personal reasons that related to the individual's personal happiness and (2) reasons that related to events or directions within the church or the order. This accounting scheme is based on the model of decision making that takes into account both personal and situation factors. Since commitment to religious life is basically a per-

Table 12. *Primary reasons for leaving*

N = 57

Personal reasons	No.	%
Marriage	5	8
Unhappiness	6	11
Self-fulfillment	10	18
Never should have entered	5	9
Subtotal	26	46
Reasons related to church or order		
Don't see value in canonical religious life	8	13
Job dissatisfaction	4	6
Order changing too fast	4	7
Order not changing fast enough	13	24
Other	2	4
Subtotal	31	54
Total	57	100

sonal commitment to live and serve within a well-defined context, it seemed essential to take into account both the personal commitment dimension and the changing nature of the organizational context, especially in these post–Vatican II times of renewal and change.

Analysis of the reasons women gave for leaving their religious orders shows that 31 women (54%) left because of events in their orders or in the Catholic Church while 26 (46%) left for personal reasons (see table 12). For the group of interviewees as a whole, therefore, almost equal numbers gave personal reasons and reasons related to the order. The important question for the present study, however, is whether these reasons vary randomly among those leaving all orders or whether reasons cluster by order.

When primary reasons for leaving are analyzed by order from which interviewees left, clear-cut patterns emerge. As table 13 shows, approximately three-fourths of the women who left orders A and C left for reasons related to events in the church or order while 85% of those who left Order B left because of personal reasons. Analysis of variance shows that these interorganizational differences are statistically significant.

Even though the reasons women left both the liberal order (Order A) and the conservative order (Order C) are related to what was going on

Table 13. *Primary reasons for leaving by order*

N = 57

	Order A No.	Order A %	Order B No.	Order B %	Order C No.	Order C %
Personal reasons						
Marriage	2	10	3	17	0	0
Unhappiness	1	5	4	21	1	5
Self-fulfillment	2	10	4	21	4	20
Never should have entered	0	0	5	26	0	0
Subtotal	5	25	16	85	5	25
Reasons related to church or order						
Don't see value in canonical religious life	7	39	1	5	0	0
Job dissatisfaction	4	21	0	0	0	0
Order changing too fast	2	10	2	10	0	0
Order not changing fast enough	0	0	0	0	13	70
Other	1	5	0	0	1	5
Subtotal	14	75	3	15	14	75
Total	19	100	19	100	19	100

in the larger context of church and religious life, the two groups differed greatly in their reasons. Thirteen, or 70%, of the women who left Order C left because of lack of change in the order. Of all the reasons given by the 57 interviewees, this is the largest percentage in any one category. While the reasons given by those from Order A are less clustered, none left because change was too slow and only 2 because it was too fast. Seven women, or 39%, left Order A for reasons related to ideological, doctrinal, or theological changes, compared with none from Order C and only one from Order B. In other words, as predicted in Hypotheses V and VI, over one-third of the women left the liberal order because of reasons related to the basic legitimation of religious life while over two-thirds left the conservative order because of lack of changes in the order.

Hypothesis VII predicted that more women would have left Order B for personal reasons than left for personal reasons in either of the other orders. Of the 26 who gave personal reasons as primary in their decision to leave, 16, or 61%, were women from Order B. In fact, 85% of all the interviewees who left Order B gave some personal reason as primary in their decision. Only 3 listed reasons related to the order, and one of these said that the structures of religious life prevented her personal growth.

Significantly more women who left Order B were married or engaged at the time of the interview than from either Orders A or C. Eight from Order B were married and 2 were engaged compared with 5 married and none engaged from Order C and only 2 married from Order A. This further substantiates the fact that women from Order B were concerned with personal issues.

On the basis of the primary reasons given for leaving, therefore, patterns are very pronounced. The majority of women left the conservative order because of the slow pace of change; over 60% left the moderate-change order because of personal reasons; and about one-third left the liberal order because they no longer believed in the basic goals of religious life.

In addition to the primary reason for leaving, each interviewee was asked if there were any other reasons that might have motivated her decision. Analysis of these secondary reasons reinforces and strengthens the general findings based on primary reasons. Most interviewees from Order C listed lack of change as both primary and secondary reason for their leaving. In Order A, in addition to the 7 women giving theological or goal-related reasons as primary for their leaving, 6 listed such reasons as secondary in their decision. Considering primary reason and secondary reason together, 5 women from Order A disagreed with official church positions and did not wish to be publicly identified with the church. Eight felt that changing theology showed that religious life is not necessarily the most viable way to serve the church. The pattern of women leaving Order B for personal reasons is emphasized when primary and secondary reasons are considered together since 17 of the 19 women listed personal reasons as part of why they left.

The following comments from women who had left each order illustrate differences in reasons for leaving and perceptions of religious life in their respective orders. Typical among interviewees from Order A was the following comment: ''I didn't believe in the system of religious life enough to put my energies there. Things had opened up so much that there wasn't too much meaning in the sacrifices of the life and you could do basically the same things outside as you did in the life. My basic commitment is the same as before and so is my obedience. What I have now and didn't before is the legal freedom to marry. I may never marry but I wanted the legal freedom to do so if I ever met the right man." Another put it this way: "I felt I was on a sinking ship and wanted to get out where I didn't have to struggle to find meaning for my life." Repeatedly throughout the interviews with ex-members from Order A was the comment that there isn't too much difference any more between religious life and a lay life and that therefore there was no longer sufficient reason to stay, especially with the sacrifices celibacy demanded. Frequent mention was made of the council's document on the ministry of the laity and the need for Christian lay women who could live an exemplary life as wife and mother.

Comments from women from Order B were very different from those of Order A's ex-members; however, *within* the Order B group they were also very similar. Many women stressed the mentality that pervaded their early novitiate training and militated against any thought of not being faithful to the "call." As one woman put it, "I never should have entered. It took me twenty years to realize that. But I went right through parochial school so entering religious life was no big decision. Once you entered you simply wouldn't leave. There was only one direction, one path, and you wouldn't think of leaving. That was just temptation from the devil. However, I never was happy and finally I got a sickness brought on by tensions and stress and my psychiatrist showed me I had to get out." Part of the novitiate emphasis that supported a fear of leaving was stress on the conception of the Providence of God and the importance of doing God's will in all things. One woman expressed it in this way, "I always wanted to leave but we were brainwashed in the idea that God wants me here. What *I* wanted was not important but what God wants. I entered because religious life was presented as the best way to live. I felt constantly guilty because I was not happy. I probably never had a vocation. In fact, my vows probably weren't even valid."

As structural and theological changes occurred in the order, the phenomenon of leaving lost much of the social stigma formerly associated with it. Concomitantly, within the larger Catholic community and in society in general, it became more and more common to know someone who had once been a Catholic nun. Greater social acceptance of women who left the convent made it easier for nuns to entertain the option of leaving. This freedom encouraged nuns to rethink their original commitment and face the possibility that they really were not happy as nuns.

Among the leavers from Order C, many comments indicated bitterness toward the order, especially toward the conservative administration. Also typical was the remark that the person really did not want to leave religious life but the rigid position of the order made it impossible for her to stay. A typical statement was, "Renewal was a dirty word to the administration. They maintained the order had existed for 115 years and would be a model of religious life. Committed Christians, they kept saying, are the religious of today. Their position was that there is no need for large orders and that all 'undesirables' and 'malcontents' should leave so that those left would be good religious." Or, as another put it, "I never questioned religious life per se, only the form of that life as it was happening in our order. I did not really want to leave the community but I couldn't accept the rigid form of government that existed and was refusing to change, even with renewal in the church. Authority rested in the personality of whoever was in office and the mother general could appoint who she could work with. There was no consultation or asking the sisters for suggestions."

In general, therefore, women leaving each of the three orders were very homogeneous not only in their reasons for severing membership but also in their perceptions of experience in the order, how the particular order compared with other orders, and how attuned it was to the whole renewal process occurring within the Catholic Church.

Analysis of reasons for leaving by age, occupation, educational background, and academic field, both for the sample as a whole and for individual orders, showed no systematic differences. Detailed comparisons and analyses were made, especially of those women who had master's degrees and doctorates compared with those women with only B.A. degrees. However, no patterns or associations were evident between reasons for leaving and amount of education. Even the factor of greater association with seculars during graduate study did not significantly affect differences in reasons for leaving. This fact supports the finding presented in chapter four that the educational experience of individuals had less effect upon their personal decisions than it did in creating an organizational climate where members in general questioned their commitment and where leaving became more acceptable than in the former system.

In the 1970 study on priestly life and the ministry sponsored by the Catholic Conference of Bishops, the primary reason for leaving given both by priests who had left the ministry and those who intended to leave was the desire to marry. This reason took precedence over dissatisfaction with events in the church or diocese, job dissatisfaction, or seeing priestly life as no longer relevant. Among women leaving, however, the desire to marry was not articulated as a predominant influence. The data on the number who had actually married since leaving support the fact that marriage is not a major factor. Many of the women who had been out of the order for three years or more still had not married and did not intend to do so.

In addition to questions on why the person left the order, the interview schedule included questions regarding the kinds of influences that affected her decision—specifically, about policy decisions in the order; friends; church proclamations; exposure to new ideas while studying; associations while away from the order; family; seeing a psychiatrist, priest, or counselor; and mass media. The interviewee was asked which of these influences were most important as she began questioning and at a later stage in questioning whether there were any decisive factors that helped her make her decision.

As might be expected, the influences of most importance in each order are in keeping with the pattern of responses to reasons people left. In Order C, for example, the lack of change effected by the administration influenced the majority of interviewees at all three stages in the decision process. Friends in the order, predominantly those themselves in the process of leaving, had an effect on 6 women in their decision to exit.

In Order B, the single most important influence that led to initial questioning was the personal unhappiness of the individual herself, 14 interviewees listing this as the factor that first prodded them to doubt their own commitment. Only 3 persons mentioned this factor as important in the intermediary stage, but 12 said that their own unhappiness was what finally prompted them to leave. Three women in Order B mentioned the advice of a psychiatrist as an important factor during their decision-making process.

Influences of importance to interviewees in Order A during all three stages of decision making were much more varied than for either of the other two groups. In the initial stage, exposure to changing theological thought influenced 3 women to begin questioning. Two others said that coming into contact with all types of new ideas and thinking while away studying led them to reevaluate religious life for themselves. Friends, both those within the order and those who had already left, influenced 7 of the interviewees at different stages in their decision. Two women who left primarily because of a dissatisfaction with job opportunities in the order said that a decision by the order in this respect was the initial factor influencing them to question their commitment.

Attitudes toward renewal and changes in their former order, degree of emotional identification with the order, and amount of association with members of the order also varied for women in each order. Women from Order A were, on the whole, most positive toward the order while those from Order C were negative and those from Order B either neutral or negative.

Despite the fact that the interviewees had severed their formal relationships with the order, it was common for Order A's ex-members to express satisfaction with the direction and pace of change in the order. Two women felt that the changes had been too fast and too radical; however, the remaining 17 expressed support of the changes, and many of them said they had taken an active part in bringing them about.

In contrast, 14 of the 19 interviewees from Order C were hostile toward their former order, especially toward the present administration, which had publicly taken a conservative position toward change. In addition to strong negative feelings toward the order, there was frequently a sense that injustice had been done those who left. This sense of injustice was further intensified by feelings that the administration had caused some people to give up a religious calling against the individual's own free choice. The idea that many people who left Order C never had the opportunity to make a personal decision regarding their future in religious life was frequently mentioned. An indication that this in fact was the case was the anxiety in many of the interviewees from Order C.

Two of the interviewees from Order B left because they felt the order was changing too fast and in the wrong direction. However, none of the other 17 leavers said that the changes in the order affected their decision to leave in any direct way, except that individuals were now free to think for themselves and about themselves and were free to leave if they felt it would make them happier. When asked if and how changes in the order affected their decision to leave, the majority said that it wouldn't have mattered what changes were or were not made, they would have left anyway.

At the same time, however, a majority of the interviewees from Order B expressed concern and some even strong negative feelings that some of the changes were going too far. As one put it, "I just don't like to see nuns in bars and street clothes. You can't even tell who is a nun anymore." Another woman was concerned about what would draw young people in the future if all the sacrifice and distinctiveness were gone from the life. "I wouldn't want to be in now. They're not doing any more than I am. They should wear something distinctive and be proud to be a nun. They shouldn't be in bars, etc., where men don't know who they are. It's supposed to be a life of dedication. It drew people before. Now it doesn't. You used to be something different but what are the goals of the order now? Why should young people enter? Now you don't give up anything and there's no community any more. You still need some sign and some community prayers. But now it's become a nothing life.'' A typical response was, ''Religious orders have to change, but where are they going?''

While the majority of interviewees from Order A supported the changes effected by the order and felt that the order was moving in the right direction, the majority from Order B expressed fear and regret that the changes would result in the end of an identifiable religious life. Interviewees from Order C were angry toward the order for lack of change, which they saw as a rigid position forcing people to leave.

As far as continued association with members of the order, ex-members from Order A had the greatest amount of association. In fact, 2 of the 19 women were living at the time with members of the order and 6 were working with present members. The majority of interviewees had periodic contact with members. There was also a tendency among Order A's ex-members to maintain some contact with others who had left, not through a formal association but through friendships that had been established while in the order. In fact, 13 of the 19 women said they often associated with others who had left the order and only 2 said they never had such associations.

Only 4 out of the 19 leavers from Order B maintained any kind of association with women still in the order. There was also little contact among women who had left. Only 4 of the 19 associated often with others who had left, and 5 never saw anyone else who had left. This may be due to the fact that more women from Order B were married or engaged and had established heterogeneous social circles than leavers from either of the other two orders.

Among the women from Order C there was much contact both with women still in the order and especially among the ex-members themselves. In fact, a striking network existed among the majority of those who had left. Strong feelings of solidarity existed, and it was common for ex-members to get together frequently, both formally and informally. I was present at one of these get-togethers. The principal topic of conversation was the former order and how unjust the situation was and remains. Feelings of loyalty toward the order were obviously replaced by loyalty to the group who had left, and cohesion was maintained by the feeling that the group had been ousted by the order. When an individual left the order, this group assisted her in getting established on the outside. It served, therefore, as an intermediary between life in the order and an independent existence in the wider society.

In summary, striking similarities in reasons for leaving and attitudes toward religious life existed among women from the same order who had left. Just as bold are the differences that existed among leavers from the three different orders. Many women who left the liberal order had been instrumental in effecting change in the order; however, after radical changes had been initiated, many of them began to question the basic goals of religious life and decided that these goals no longer justified the costs of membership.

Women from Order B left for personal reasons and not because of change or lack of it in the order. While many regretted the loss of public identity and uniqueness of religious in contemporary society, they were also grateful for the changed attitude toward leaving which facilitated their own decision to exit. Few women from Order B kept in contact with either members of the order or other ex-members.

Order C's ex-members were, on the whole, bitter toward the order and held the administration responsible for causing them to leave the order because of their rigid and conservative position. Ex-members formed a strong group with frequent interaction and high cohesiveness and reinforced a sense of injustice on the part of the order. Many women from Order C felt that they were not really given an opportunity to make a personal decision regarding their leaving the order since it was impossible to tolerate policy decisions and actions of the reactionary administration in the order.

Reasons for Staying

Why are some women opting to remain in the order while others are leaving? Do the women who stay differ in experience or attitudes from those who leave? What goal or purpose do the "stayers" see for religious life? In order to answer these questions, interviews were conducted with 26 women, 10 who were still members in Order A, 10 in Order B, and 6 in Order C. Because of the existing tensions in Order C, it was possible to interview only 6 persons. However, these 6 were representative of the order in age, occupation, and educational background. One among them was in the current administration but was on the verge of leaving the order because of the injustices she saw within the administration.

The sample of "stayers" is too small to justify any firm conclusions. However, it does provide some insight into different orientations and perceptions on the part of those who left and those who stayed.

Areas that were of special interest during the interviews with women still in religious orders were: why the individual was choosing to remain in the order, what she saw as the future of religious life in the church, and what issues she thought were most important in her order at the moment. Again, as in the case of the "leavers," interviewees were most cooperative and eager to talk about where they saw religious life in general and what it meant to them personally within their own orders.

In Order A the most common response to the question of why they were staying was a belief in the value of a group of women dedicated to witnessing Christianity in the world. This "witnessing" was frequently related to involvement in social issues, such as taking public stances on civil rights issues, political campaigning, involvement in the Equal Rights Amendment movement, and active support of equal job opportunities for minorities. Many women in Order A felt strongly that involvement in social issues should be a corporate goal and not just a matter of individual effort. If the order as a corporate group committed itself to alleviating social problems, a stronger public stance could be taken on important social questions.

The most commonly used phrases throughout the interview with members of Order A were corporate commitment, corporate thrusts, sense of the whole, sense of the purpose of our community, and corporate goals. This concern with defining the corporate value or task of the order was, in part, a reaction to the personalism that was a hallmark of legislation and philosophy during the three or four years since the initiation of renewal in the order. As one person put it, "The whole thrust of personalism is great but we have no background and responsibility for it. Now there is overstress on the person." And another, "The key issue at the moment is a sense of community in terms of the whole. We've spent enough time reorganizing and being individuals and now we are ready to think about community." While the order was emphasizing personalism and self-determination, several people felt there was insufficient attention given to the goals of the institution and the tasks at hand. As one said, "The institutions and commitments are moving from under us. We need corporate commitments; there are values in this." And another, "What is our apostolate? Where is our cohesiveness? We're all in this together but what does it effect?"

Another concern for several members was the deepening of a faith and prayer life in the order. These women felt that, in the shuffle of restructuring, the order had "gotten away from" the need for being women of deep faith. As one person said, "Religious life is not just an intellectual thing or a humanistic venture. It is a faith life and this takes effort."

A vital concern for women in Order A, therefore, was for the community to define a corporate apostolic goal and begin to stress the value of being part of a faith community. Many members felt that personalism and individual freedom were overstressed during renewal and that now equal emphasis needed to be placed upon the value of group belonging. Data on why members left the group support this concern of members since the majority of women who left Order A did so because they no longer saw the group as resourceful or beneficial.

In Order B both the reasons women were staying and the issues and concerns that were considered foremost in the order were more varied than for the other two orders. Six women were staying for individually oriented reasons, 2 because they were happy in the order, and the other 4 for reasons that touched upon religious motivation. Two of the 4 favored the order's remaining in the traditional apostolates of teaching, nursing, and social work. The other 2 expressed a desire for more contemporary apostolic thrusts, such as political involvement and more direct service to underprivileged groups.

Unlike members in Order A, members in Order B felt that the order had defined a corporate thrust and that emphasis had been placed all along on what the group could offer the individual. The majority of members interviewed expressed concern that the order assist individuals in such areas of personal growth as adjustment to change and effective small-group living. In addition, there was a pervading emphasis among Order B's members that religious life is basically a faith life, that prayer and faith commitment must be the primary focus of the order, and that all changes have to be made with religious goals in mind. Since women in Order B felt that the order had emphasized the value of group belonging and now needed to focus more upon the personal growth and adaptation of individual members, this raises the question of whether Order B can emphasize greater personalism without jeopardizing a sense of group solidarity and meaning.

All 6 of the women interviewed in Order C were experiencing frustration in the order. Speaking informally with others in the order during a visit to the convent, I noted that this feeling of frustration and discouragement seemed to be the prevalent mood of the younger members, that is, those under 50. It was a time, therefore, when a number of those still in the order were requestioning their commitment.

In addition to the generally conservative position of the present administration, an event occurred during the week of interviewing that upset many people. The previous May each member was asked to indicate her job preference for the following September. When assignments were publicized, however, there was little or no indication that attention had been given to these preferences. When individuals approached the administration asking for explanations of their assignments, they were told, "Take your assignment in obedience or leave." Five members did leave the week the interviews were conducted, specifically because of this event in the order.

Two of those "stayers" who were interviewed planned to leave the order soon. One of these was then a member of the general administration who felt that she could no longer condone the injustices that she felt were going on at the administrative level. She herself was being ostracized by the rest of the administration because she refused to conform to the policies set by the majority.

The idea that injustices were going on within the order toward certain members was prevalent among the interviewees. Such injustices were being done to those whose preferences and needs were not being considered in job assignments, those who felt they had to leave because of lack of change, and the administrator who was informally being ousted from office. As one person said, "The big issue is the injustices in the administration and people not having enough freedom to do what they see as important. In a few years, even those alive ones left will leave." The predominant tone both on the part of women who had left the order and those still in was that the institution was dying. Yet, some did remain in the order. Three of the 6 interviewed were dedicated to the work they were doing and felt they could not do the work as well outside religious life. One of these was principal of a large high school, and she felt the school was serving the needs of youth. The other 2 were involved in social work and felt that the habit and their being called "sister" gave them privileged access to certain homes and areas of the city. All 3, however, made it clear that the order did not interfere with their work and that, if this situation were to change, they would have to reconsider their membership.

One older woman admitted that she was staying for the sake of security, which she felt she was too old to establish in a new situation. However, she feared that no one would be left to care for her when she retired.

The women who were in the process of deciding to leave were still evaluating the events of the past few months. As one said, "We went back 30 years in the last two months. Now assignments are made with no consultation and some people are forced out and not by their own free choice.''

In general, the climate in Order C was very pessimistic. Those who were staying were older members who supported the conservative position of the administration and women who felt their work was still meaningful within the order or who needed the security provided by the group.

Women in Order B were generally happy about the direction of change in the order and were staying because they believed in its meaning and purposes. Emphasis in the order was primarily upon assisting individuals to grow both in their own persons and in the context of the local group in which they were living.

The predominant reason individuals were staying in Order A was to be part of a corporate effort to witness Christianity and serve the needs of deprived people. A primary concern of women in Order A was the need for the order to articulate a corporate thrust which would give meaning to belonging.

In general, women who were opting to remain in their religious orders felt that membership in the order was conducive to the type of work or life-style they wanted. Two values of membership in religious orders that were emphasized were support for a faith commitment, including a community to pray with, and a corporate thrust in apostolic work.

6. Convents: Reflections on Their Present and Future

When Pope Pius XII spoke in 1952 to the superiors general of religious women from all over the world and instructed them to educate the members of their institutes on a par with other professionals, he no doubt did not anticipate the profound, far-reaching ramifications of compliance with his mandate. In the same vein, the renewal and adaptation called for by the council fathers at Vatican II resulted in changes so radical in religious orders that it is doubtful that some of them will survive the change process. Organizations which historically exemplified total institutions in which members were cut off from the larger society and lived in a highly uniform, centralized, and depersonalized style of life were suddenly changed into organizations that valued personal initiative, individual responsibility, and decentralization of authority.

While changes were occurring within the central structures of religious orders—such as increased contact with out-group members, the removal of outward signs of membership in the group (uniforms, rings, crosses, etc.), individual choice in job and living situations and greater financial independence—the central structure of celibacy remained. As greater personalism and a sense of self-identity were emphasized in religious orders, and as the exalted status of nuns in the Catholic Church was deemphasized by the official church and by the laity, the costs of membership in a religious order increased in relation to the rewards of membership for some members.

Typical of utopian groups is the total commitment of the individual to the group and the discovery of personal identity in the identity of the group. As studies of utopian groups show, the success of the group depends upon the total and complete identification of individual identity with that of the group and the sacrifice of individual needs and wants to collective goals.

One mechanism utilized by utopian groups to achieve commitment to group goals and the merging of individual identity with the collective is strict boundary maintenance, whereby members are segregated from the outside. Daily association and social contact, therefore, are limited to group members. Such isolation reduces the possibility that group members will take on reference groups outside the community and become identified with goals that are in conflict with group goals.

The changes that have occurred in religious orders during the past decade of renewing and adapting to contemporary conditions have occurred primarily in boundary-maintaining structures. Not only was the proscription of contact with outsiders changed so that fewer sanctions were brought to bear upon members who entered into associations with out-group members, but such contact with outsiders came to be positively valued as part of a renewed sense of apostolate and witness. Differences between members and nonmembers were formally deemphasized in an attempt to improve communication between members and those outsiders they wanted to influence.

As a result of this changed emphasis, however, and more lenient rules regarding association in the larger society, some members began to calculate the costs and rewards of group membership in terms other than total commitment of self to the group. As data in the present study show, some group members began to ask whether the costs of belonging to the group were compensated for by rewards of group membership. Particularly in the liberal order that was studied, some women began to feel that they could achieve the same goals for their life outside the order without having to pay the main price of membership, namely, celibacy. Other women, particularly those in the moderate-change order, began to realize that they had made a total commitment of self to the group but that it had been done under various types of psychological pressures and that they really were not happy in the order and were not obtaining the types of personal rewards that would make their life happy and fulfilled. Until religious orders accepted the fact that individual happiness was valuable and lessened the sanctions of leaving the group, these women did not question their own happiness, at least not publicly, but continued to identify with the group.

The very way in which members of religious orders began to calculate the value of membership in cost and reward terms is an indication of the changed nature of these groups. In the former system, as in most utopias, commitment was a zero-sum game in which the individual gave herself totally to the group, renouncing personal desires, and in return gained the security and sense of belonging which a strong group identity provided. Constant interaction with group members reinforced by respect and awe on the part of outsiders caused members not to question the value of being one of the group. However, in the "renewed" orders, where collective identity was weakened and association with out-group members increased, more and more women began to weigh the resources and benefits of group membership against the concomitant costs.

Such cost-benefit calculations are characteristic of voluntary associations in which groups of people join together in segmental areas of their lives to achieve goals that are impossible or at least more difficult to achieve alone. The role of the organization, therefore, is to provide resources for the individual members to achieve whatever goals they want to accomplish or to provide meaningful collective goals for individual members.

Data in the present study from both members and ex-members indicate that religious orders are being perceived more and more in terms of the unique resources they can provide. The sample of women who opted to stay felt that the order could offer resources to individual members that are not available in the larger society, particularly in terms of corporate apostolic thrusts and incentives for personal growth. Those who decided to leave their orders judged that the costs of membership outweighed the benefits that the order could provide.

If it is true that religious orders have changed from utopian type groups to voluntary organizations, there are numerous policy implications that religious orders might well take into account in planning change. The most important of these is that the orders must be able to provide meaningful resources to their members. Data in this study suggest that there are two major areas where members are looking to the order for guidance and assistance, first, to assist their own personal growth and development, and second, to provide meaningful corporate goals that can be achieved more effectively by a group than by lone individuals. Both of these areas also assume that the order can develop ways of assuring individuals that membership in the group is valuable. The type of solidarity mechanisms that are appropriate for voluntary organizations are different from those in utopian groups but are nevertheless just as essential for the survival of the group. Perhaps the greatest challenge to religious orders in their post–Vatican II modality is to discover how they can structure commitment mechanisms and a sense of group solidarity and belongingness when members are more and more diversified in job, life-style, recreation, finance, and dress.

The processes that have occurred within religious orders during the past several decades involve numerous organizational dilemmas which make policy change especially challenging. A dilemma is essentially a choice between equally undesirable alternatives. Sometimes a dilemma is anticipated in advance and choice is made on the basis of which alternative seems more advantageous. At other times, however, as Merton has pointed out, consequences are not anticipated in advance but are realized only after action has occurred.[1] Most of the dilemmas experienced by religious orders in the change process were unanticipated when policy changes were made. Or, if outcomes were anticipated by some individuals in the order, they did not get articulated in a way that would force policy makers to take them into account in making decisions. Rather, organizational moves were made with immediate outcomes in mind or under the mandate of a higher authority without consideration of long-term effects.

One of the dilemmas within religious orders was the emphasis upon increased educational preparation on the part of members. In an attempt to improve professional competence so as to comply with the mandate of the pope, educational levels within religious orders soared during the late 1950's and early 1960's. Therefore, orders with substantial numbers of educated women heard and responded to the call for change made by the bishops during Vatican Council II. The scope and rapidity with which orders in the United States responded to the call toward change surprised even the church hierarchy. Not only were church officials surprised, but in several instances they disapproved of the nature and extent of the changes effected. Once Pope John "opened the windows" and allowed the winds of change to enter the church, the results in some orders far surpassed what the church officials had in mind when they encouraged religious orders of women to question and reevaluate every aspect of their life-style.

Data in the present study show that educational level in an order is the best predictor of the degree of structural change effected in the order. In other words, those religious orders that had a high proportion of educated women initiated greater structural change than the orders that had fewer women equipped with master's degrees. One of the consequences, therefore, of bettering educational backgrounds of religious women was the creation of a type of religious community that looked very different from its earlier counterpart, especially in the degree of individual initiative, personalism, and decentralization that was effected in the order.

At the same time, educational level in an order is also a predictor of increasing rates of leaving from religious orders. Not only did increasing rates of education lead to greater change, but at the same time those orders in which greater numbers of women had master's degrees experienced the greatest rates of exodus from the order. Interestingly, however, it was not only those who had acquired the higher degrees who departed but also members who were less well-educated. This finding indicates that in some way rising educational levels changed the general milieu of the order in such a way as to cause the less-educated members as well as the educated to question their commitment and opt to leave the renewed order.

Another dilemma that religious orders faced during the change process was related to the reason increasing numbers of women opted to leave. As data in chapter five indicate, in the order where much change occurred, women left because there was no longer sufficient reason to stay, that is, the value of group membership no longer outweighed the cost of staying. In the conservative order, women left because no change occurred and the prospects for change looked bleak indeed. In the order where moderate change prevailed, women also left, in this instance because they came to realize that they just weren't happy in the order and would not be regardless of the changes made or not made.

The dilemma created for the orders in these reasons for leaving is that women opted to leave the order regardless of policy actions on the part of the order. It was as if it did not matter what the order did—the phenomenon of increasing numbers leaving persisted. At the same time, the increasing numbers leaving, especially on the part of younger members, coupled with decreasing numbers entering meant that median ages were rising in orders, and the number of those who normally would be the future of the order dwindled. In many instances, this led to declining morale in the order.

One of the basic reasons underlying the evolution of organizational dilemmas in religious orders during the process of renewal and change was that structural and value change was effected without a concomitant change in organizational goals. Religious orders continued to define themselves in terms of teaching, nursing, and social work as ways of glorifying God and serving the church even though the need for these services had changed in modern society. Parochial institutions, for example, in which the vast majority of religious women work, have undergone drastic role changes. It is no longer mandatory for Catholic parents to send their children to Catholic schools. The ever-increasing burden of a private school education, as costs continue to rise each year, has meant that the parochial school population has decreased.

Concomitantly, increasing numbers of religious women began to question the value of their service within Catholic institutions, especially in the instances where parochial schools were providing inferior educations to state-supported institutions. Many nuns began asking what teaching math, English, or science had to do with their religious commitment and began opting, in the era of greater choice in job placement, to go into works that are more directly involved in religious education or serving the poor.

In addition, nuns began to realize that the government also has the goal of providing education, hospital care, and social services for the American people. What, then, makes the goal of religious life distinct enough to call forth a life commitment from individuals? What can belonging to a religious order do for a person and for an individual's contribution to society that remaining a lay person cannot? Since 1970 the number of nuns teaching in Catholic schools has declined rapidly, due to the increasing numbers leaving their orders and to the fact that many nuns are choosing work outside of the Catholic school system. As a result, Catholic schools have hired more and more lay teachers to staff the schools. In 1950, for example, there were 82,048 nuns who taught in Catholic schools compared with 13,477 lay teachers, approximately 6 nuns for every 1 lay teacher. By 1960 the ratio was about equal, one nun for every lay teacher. By 1975, the ratio had reversed from the decade of the 1950's, and there were about 2 lay teachers for every 1 nun in the schools.[2] One consequence of this shift is the increasing cost of Catholic school education since lay teachers typically demand higher salaries than nuns.

The Vatican Council fathers, in their document on religious life, assumed that religious orders would maintain their same goals, and the mandate given to religious orders was to reevaluate and create those structural changes necessary in order to achieve their traditional goals more effectively. What happened, however, was that in the process of reevaluation religious women began to question the appropriateness of the goals themselves. Also, there was no systematic effort in most orders to come to terms with changing goals and to assure that members agreed on basic goals before introducing structural changes. The result was that uncertainty and disagreement existed regarding the goals of the organization while, simultaneously, structural changes were being initiated with little systematic questioning of how such structural changes related to goals. Merton refers to the process of means becoming ends in themselves as that of "the displacement of goals."[3] In the case of religious orders, structures were being changed rapidly, and the change process itself created excitement and temporary commitment from some members. However, after the structural changes lost some of their newness and people became used to the newly institutionalized structures, more and more religious women began questioning the relationship between renewed structures and nebulous goals. Since most of the changes were in the direction of greater personal freedom and initiative, the central question of the unique goals of religious life became more and more an issue for many nuns.

Interview data from both members and ex-members indicate that the most tenuous and challenging area for religious orders presently is a redefinition of organizational goals, especially in terms of apostolic commitments. Uniformity in jobs and a sense of making a Catholic school system possible and Catholic hospitals feasible were central commitment mechanisms in the pre–Vatican II orders. Solidarity and unity were achieved by members in their service goals. The solidarity mechanisms that are appropriate for the type of voluntary organization that characterizes contemporary orders are different from those in the former system. However, a sense of solidarity and group belonging-ness is just as critical for a sense of commitment to the group. It is perhaps time for religious orders to undergo a succession of goals and to discover a unique role for themselves in the current church and larger world. While teaching and nursing were primary needs of an immigrant, rural church in eighteenth and nineteenth century America, issues which are just as real and poignant in today's church might well be the needs of minority groups and the white poor and the political and radical injustices prevalent in society. Or, perhaps, it is time for American religious women to begin to look beyond highly indus-trialized, technological America, where the government has taken over many of the functions previously carried out by private religious groups, and to think in terms of service to the Third World, where the impact of a group of highly committed, dedicated women could be dramatically felt.

It is also possible that religious orders will need to refocus their goals away from service tasks and toward an emphasis upon creating a supportive community for members. There is indication in contempo-rary orders that such a change in emphasis is actually occurring. The goal of religious orders, therefore, becomes group centered rather than service oriented. What members do jobwise becomes far less important than their sharing together a supportive group life that meets the needs of the members. When this occurs, religious orders become part of the larger commutarian movement increasingly evident in the Western world in the past decade.

Appendices

1. Organizational Surveys

June, 1971

1. What is the governmental structure of the order? (Please check).
   _____International order _____National administration with provinces
   _____National administration with no provinces _____Other:_____
   If an international order, in what country is the general administration located?
   _____
   If a national order with provinces, in what state is the general administration located? _____
2. In what year was the order founded? _____
   In what country was the order founded? _____
3. In what year did the first sisters in the order come to the U.S.? _____
4. Size of order: _____ If an international order, size of membership in the United States: _____ If provinces, size of your province: _____
   FOR THE FOLLOWING QUESTIONS, IF YOU ARE AN ORDER WITH NO PROVINCES, PLEASE ANSWER FOR THE ENTIRE ORDER; IF YOU ARE AN ORDER WITH PROVINCES, PLEASE ANSWER FOR YOUR PROVINCE.
5. List your primary apostolates:
6. What is the ethnic background of the majority of sisters? (Check one).
   _____Irish _____German _____French _____Polish _____Spanish
   _____Italian _____Mexican _____Black _____Other:_____
7. What was the median age of your membership in each of the following years?
   1960:_____ 1967:_____ 1970:_____
8. How many women entered the novitiate in each of the following years?
   1960:_____ 1965:_____ 1970:_____
9. When was your renewal chapter held? Month_____ Year_____
10. In what year was the present administration elected? Central:_____
    Provincial:_____
11. Which of the following most closely describes communal prayer in the order?
    _____Strictly an individual matter _____Determined by local communities
    _____Uniform within the order _____Other:_____
12. Can sisters choose those persons with whom they want to live?
    Yes_____ No_____
    If "Yes," under what conditions? Please describe:
13. At present, how many sisters hold: M.A.'s or equivalent? _____
    Ph.D.'s or equivalent? _____

14. How do sisters obtain jobs? (Check as many of the following as are applicable in order of frequency, e.g., #1, 2, 3.)
_____assignment by the central administration _____assignment by a personnel commission   _____openings are advertised by the administration or personnel commission and individuals apply _____openings are advertised by the diocese and individuals apply _____individuals seek out their own jobs through public channels   _____Other:_____

15. Check any of the following administrative commissions or committees presently operative and indicate the year they were established.
_____religious life (Yr._____) _____spiritual life (Yr._____)
_____personnel (Yr._____) _____apostolic works (Yr._____)
_____planning and development (Yr._____) _____public relations
(Yr._____) _____formation (Yr._____) _____research (Yr._____)
_____finance (Yr._____) _____Other:_____

16. How many sisters requested dispensations, leaves of absence, exclaustrations, or did not renew annual vows in the following years?

Yr.	Dispensations, leaves of absence, exclaustrations for finally professed	Expiration of annual vows
1960		
1961		
1962		
1963		
1964		
1965		
1966		
1967		
1968		
1969		
1970		
1971		

17. How many sisters returned after leaves of absence or exclaustrations during the past ten years? _____

18. Of those who were delegates or *ex officio* members of chapters between 1966–71, how many have left? _____

19. How many finally professed sisters in the following age groups withdrew in 1960, 1964, 1968 and 1970?

Age	1960	1964	1968	1970
−30				
30–39				
40–49				
50–59				
60 & above				

20. In the past ten years how many sisters left with a M.A. or its equivalent as their highest degree in the following fields?
_____Biological, Physical and Mathematical Sciences _____Social and

Behavioral Sciences _____Humanities (including Philosophy and Art)
_____Business and Administration _____Social Work _____Education
_____Other:_____

21. Answer the following for _each_ sister with a Ph.D. or its equivalent as her highest degree who left in the past ten years (1960–1971).

Yr. of departure	Age at departure	Yr. Ph.D. received	Academic field	University attended

---

SURVEY II

October, 1971

Please answer the following questions for your entire order in the U.S., if possible; if you are a U.S. province with a motherhouse in another country, please answer for your U.S. membership. If you answer any item for a province rather than the entire order, please make an indication in the margin.

1. Upon which of the great rules is the one in your order based?
   _____St. Augustine
   _____St. Basil
   _____St. Benedict
   _____St. Vincent de Paul
   _____other; please indicate:

2. For what purposes was your order originally founded?
   _____contemplative prayer
   _____apostolic works; if so, what were they?
   Has that purpose changed radically?
   _____no
   _____yes; if yes, how has it changed:

3. Who founded your order?

4. Do your sisters take simple or solemn vows?
   _____simple
   _____solemn
   Have solemn vows ever been the custom in your order?
   _____no
   _____yes; if there has been a change in the custom, when did it occur?

5. For each year shown below, please indicate the number of sisters with permanent vows who requested dispensations (secularization), leaves of absence, or exclaustrations; for the temporary professed, indicate expiration of vows and dispensations (secularization).

Year	Finally professed			Temporary professed	
	Dispensations	Leaves of absence	Exclaustration	Expiration of vows	Dispensations
1960					
1961					
1962					
1963					
1964					
1965					
1966					
1967					
1968					
1969					
1970					
1971					

6. Of those finally professed who requested a dispensation each year, please indicate their previous status. For example, of those who requested a dispensation in 1970, how many had no previous leave or exclaustration, how many one year's leave or exclaustration, etc.?

Year	1st request (no previous leave or exclaustration)	After leave or exclaustration of 1 year	After leave or exclaustration of 2 years	After leave or exclaustration of more than 2 years
1960				
1961				
1962				
1963				
1964				
1965				
1966				
1967				
1968				
1969				
1970				
1971				

7. Are there any "fundamental" or "special" virtues which your constitutions or custom books encouraged as characteristics of sisters in your order?
   _____no
   _____yes; what are they:
8. Are there any particular feastdays or devotions which have historically been celebrated in a special way in your order (e.g., feast of St. Anne, devotion to the Infant Jesus, etc.)?
9. What are the present *formal* regulations in your order regarding dress?
   _____everyone should wear a long habit and a veil

_____ everyone should wear a uniform modified habit and a veil

_____ everyone should wear some form of modified habit and a veil

_____ everyone should wear a veil but many choose to wear contemporary clothes of prescribed colors

_____ everyone should wear a veil but may wear any form of suitable contemporary clothes

_____ veils are optional and everyone may wear what she sees suitable to the occasion

_____ other; please indicate:

10. What are the general financial arrangements in your order regarding sisters' salaries?

_____ salaries are sent directly to a superior

_____ salaries are sent to the sister, who forwards the whole amount to a superior

_____ sisters receive their salary directly, keep whatever they need for budgeted expenses and turn in the remainder

_____ sisters receive their salary directly and have their own bank account out of which they pay a proportionate amount for retirement, living expenses, etc.

_____ other; please indicate:

2. Interview Schedules

INTERVIEW SCHEDULE FOR "LEAVERS"

1. Int. No._____
2. Date:_____
3. Place of interview:_____
4. Age:_____
5. Years in community with vows:_____
6. How old were you when you entered?_____
7. Were you in the aspirancy? _____ Yes _____ No
8. How many brothers and sisters do you have? _____ B. _____ S.
   Were you the oldest? _____ Yes _____ No
9. What was the religion of your father as you were growing up?
   _____ Catholic
   _____ Protestant
   _____ Jewish
   _____ No religion
10. Of your mother?
    _____ Catholic
    _____ Protestant
    _____ Jewish
    _____ No religion
11. Are there any other religious in your family?
    _____ Sister   _____ Aunt
    _____ Brother   _____ Uncle
    _____ Priest   _____ Cousin
12. Are you married, single or engaged?
    _____ Married
    _____ Single
    _____ Engaged
13. (If married) How long have you been married?_____
    When did you meet your husband? _____
14. While in the community, were you ever:
    (Dates) _____ a local superior?
            _____ in the general administration?
            _____ in Formation work?
            _____ a Chapter delegate?
15. Before you left, what was your primary occupation?
    _____

What do you do today? _____

(If change in occupation) When you left, did you plan to change your occupation? _____Yes _____No

Could you have changed your occupation without leaving the order?
_____Yes _____No

16. In leaving the community, did you ask for:
(Dates) _____Exclaustration?
        _____Leave of absence?
        _____Dispensation?

17. How long before you actually left did you begin questioning religious life for yourself? _____
_____

18. What influenced you at this time to begin questioning?
_____General Chapter?
_____Mass media?
_____Church proclamations?
_____a superior?
_____family members?
_____friends in the community?
_____friends who had left the community?
_____friends outside the community?
_____a priest friend?
_____living outside the community?
_____going away to study?
        _____educational factors?
        _____associations?

19. Did any of your close friends leave before you did?
_____Yes _____No
If so, how long before? _____
Did this affect your decision in any way? _____
Have any of your close friends left since you left?
_____Yes _____No
Do you still keep in touch? _____Yes _____No

20. What is your highest degree? _____
In what field?_____
When did you receive your degree?_____
From where?_____
Did you study only during summers or throughout the academic year?
_____summers only _____academic year
Where did you live while you were studying?_____

Who would you say were your closest friends while you were studying?
_____Sisters
_____Professors
_____Priests
_____Lay students
_____Other:_____
Do you think your educational experience influenced your decision to leave?
If so, how?

21. When did you share with your family your decision to leave?
    Did you find any member of your family helpful in the process of your decision to leave?
22. Which of these influences would you say was of *most* importance to you as you *began* questioning?
23. At a later stage in your questioning, were there any other influences which came to predominate your considerations?
24. When you finally decided to leave, were there any particular decisive factors which helped you make your decision?
25. At the time you left, what were your predominant reasons for leaving?
26. In regard to the way the order was moving relative to change when you left, did you feel that the change was fast enough? _____Yes _____No
27. How did you feel about the kind(s) of changes being made?
    _____In the right direction
    _____Superficial changes
    _____In the wrong direction
    _____Emphasis was too self-centered
    _____Not broad or radical enough
28. Did you participate in the renewal chapter in any way?
    _____Delegate
    _____On grass roots committees
    _____Consultant
    _____Other:
    Did the renewal chapter and its aftermath evoke new questions on your part?
    Was it a precipitating factor in your decision to leave?
29. Evaluate the effectiveness of the renewal chapter.
30. Were you involved in any experimental or innovative programs in the community before you left?
    _____Living groups
    _____Financial
    _____Apostolates
31. While you were in the order, did you feel your talents were being used?
32. Did you find your years in the order fulfilling to you as a person?
33. How would you evaluate religious life today?
34. Has the meaning of liturgy changed for you since you left the order?
35. Has the meaning of prayer changed for you since you left?
36. How would you characterize the theology you learned in the novitiate?
    How would you evaluate that theology today?
    What theologian has most influenced your thinking in the last few years?
37. Would you describe your present living situation?
    _____with family
    _____with other former sisters
    _____with a friend
    _____alone
    _____with former sisters and sisters
38. Have you ever considered:
    _____going back to the order?
    _____joining another order?
    _____being part of a new type of communal living?

39. Do you have any association with other women who have left the order?
    _____Yes _____No
40. Do you keep up any association with the order?
    _____Yes _____No
41. Have you joined any civic organizations since you left the order?
    _____Yes _____No
    Any new Church organization? _____Yes _____No
42. In terms of your own experience, how might communities better assist persons who are leaving?
    How does this differ from your experience?

INTERVIEW SCHEDULE FOR "STAYERS"

1. Int. No._____ 2. Date:_____ 3. Place:_____
4. Age:_____ 5. Yrs. in community with vows:_____
6. How old were you when you entered? _____
7. Aspirancy? _____Yes _____No
8. How many brothers and sisters do you have? _____B. _____S.
   Were you the oldest? _____Yes _____No
9. What was the religion of your father as you were growing up?
   _____Catholic _____Protestant _____Jewish _____No religion
10. Of your mother?
    _____Catholic _____Protestant _____Jewish _____No religion
11. Are there any other religious in your family?
    _____Sister _____Brother _____Priest _____Aunt _____Uncle _____Cousin
12. Were you ever: (give dates) _____a local superior
                                 _____in general administration
                                 _____in Formation work
                                 _____a Chapter delegate
13. Education
    Undergraduate:_____; _____; _____
                          place   degree & field   date
    Graduate: _____; _____; _____
    Did you study during summers or academic year? _____summers
                                                    _____academic yr.
    Who would you say were your closest friends while you were studying?
14. What is your present living situation?
15. Do you feel the order is changing fast enough?
    How do you feel about the kinds of changes being made?
    Evaluation of the impact of the Renewal Chapter?
16. Do you have any reflections about what the community issues and problems are at the moment? How might these be dealt with?
17. How do you view the meaning of religious life at this point in time?
18. What might be some of your own reflections regarding sisters leaving the community?
19. Have any of your close friends left? _____Yes _____No
    How did this affect you?

20. Do you have contact with any sisters who have left?
21. What are some of your reflections as to why you choose to stay?
22. How do you feel your educational experience affected some of your ideas about religious life?
23. Have your years in religious life been fulfilling to you?
24. Do you feel talents are used in the order?
25. Are you or have you been involved in any experimental programs in the community?
26. What was theology like in your novitiate?
    Have you had any further theology? What was it like?
27. What does prayer mean to you now? Liturgy?
28. Much concern has been expressed that the Church is failing to deal effectively with social issues, e.g., Viet Nam, minority groups, etc. What reflections do you have about this?

3. The Problem of Nonresponse

The problem of nonresponse or missing data faces every researcher who is dealing with survey data. In large mail surveys, the issue becomes especially acute because it is frequently impossible to administer a follow-up survey in an attempt to retrieve missing data. Even in the event that a follow-up is sent to respondents, it is almost inevitable that some respondents will not comply. (For a detailed discussion of the problem, see Frederick Stephan and Philip J. McCarthy, chapter 11, "Problems of Accessibility and Cooperation," in *Sampling Opinion: An Analysis of Survey Procedures*.)

There are various ways in which the nonresponse dilemma can be handled in data analysis. One method is to reduce the sample N to those cases in which data are complete. However, such a procedure usually results in a N that is insufficient for meaningful statistical analysis as well as a modification of the original sample such that representativeness is lost. A second method, outlined by Z. W. Birnbaum and Monroe G. Sirken ("Bias Due to Nonavailability in Sampling Surveys," *Journal of the American Statistical Association* 45 [1950]: 98–110), is a mathematical calculation of possible bias and an incorporation of this into the sampling error.

A third procedure for handling missing data is the prediction of characteristics of nonrespondents on the basis of those individuals who have responded. John A. Clausen and Robert N. Ford, for example, have used simple extrapolation procedures based on the successive returns to a mail questionnaire ("Controlling Bias in Mail Questionnaires," *Journal of the American Statistical Association* 42 [1947]: 497–511). Walter A. Henricks has given a more complex, computational procedure for accomplishing the same objectives ("Adjustments for Bias by Non-response in Mailed Surveys," *Agricultural Economic Research* 1 [1949]: 52–56). These approaches assume that there exists some sort of functional relation between the time period in which a mail questionnaire is returned and the variable to be measured in the survey. The functional relationship is estimated by graphical or computational procedures and is then used for prediction.

A fourth method is that of subsampling the nonrespondents. This method assumes that a subsample of nonrespondents is selected and surveys are readministered to that subsample. If respondents refuse to reply on the follow-up, the researcher attempts to interview the respondent personally. This technique, however, runs the risk of noncomparability of mail and interview responses. (See W. Edwards Deming, "On a Probability Mechanism to Attain an Economic Balance between the Resultant Response and the Bias of Nonresponse," *Journal of the American Statistical Association* 48 [1953]: 743–772).

In the present study, the above techniques of treating missing data were considered. Because of time and costs involved, as well as difficulty in contacting nonrespondents, the decision was made not to attempt to retrieve missing data but rather to work with available data. This option was especially appropriate since some data on most of the orders were available through the *Official Catholic Directory*, which made it possible to compare respondents and nonrespondents to ascertain any sample biases.

Since the study is one of the first organizational surveys of female religious life in the United States, it was decided to present data from as many orders as possible, even though this would necessitate, in effect, using three different samples. Therefore, in chapter three, descriptive data were based on all 287 orders that responded to Survey I. At the end of chapter three, however, when analyzing the relationship between entrance rates, departure rates, and structural change, it was necessary to reduce the N since only 184 orders responded to the second survey in which change items were asked. Chapter four focused upon the influence of educational levels and size upon change and rates of leaving. Data on education and size were available for only 103 of the orders.

An analysis of the three samples showed them to be surprisingly similar in general organizational characteristics. Therefore, it was possible to use the subsamples without radically distorting respresentativeness of the sample.

Table A-1. *Rate of master's degrees*

	Sample of 287	Sample of 184	Sample of 103
Median	20.2	20.6	19.2
Mean	30.3	62.5	19.6
S.D.	96.8	234.3	11.2

Table A-2. *Degree of structural change*

	Sample of 184		Sample of 103	
	No.	%	No.	%
0	30	20	18	20
1	36	24	24	26
2	33	21	17	19
3	38	25	23	25
4	15	10	9	10
No data	32	—	12	—
Median	1.8		1.7	
S.D.	1.3		1.3	

Note: Comparable items for this index were not included in Survey I, i.e., sample of 287.

Table A-3. *Rate of leaving*

	Sample of 184	Sample of 103
Median	6.3	6.4
Mean	7.8	7.8
S.D.	8.3	8.4

Note: Rate of leaving could not be calculated in comparative fashion for Survey I respondents, i.e., sample of 287.

Table A-4. *Average size of order*

	Sample of 287		Sample of 184		Sample of 103	
	No.	%	No.	%	No.	%
−100	54	21	62	34	9	9
100–199	44	18	29	17	25	24
200–299	30	12	20	10	16	15
300–599	59	24	37	20	30	29
600–999	31	13	18	9	12	12
1000+	30	12	18	10	11	11
No data	39	—	0	0	0	0

Table A-5. *Number of master's degrees*

	Sample of 287	Sample of 184	Sample of 103
Median	47.2	46.5	50.0
Mean	101.8	99.4	103.6
S.D.	140.3	139.3	146.4

Table A-6. *Number of Ph.D.'s*

	Sample of 287	Sample of 184	Sample of 103
Median	3.9	4.1	4.1
Mean	19.4	20.1	17.9
S.D.	31.2	33.3	30.5

The data indicate that all three samples are very similar on all organizational variables, with the exceptions of some differences between the 184 sample and 103 sample on size and rate of education. Significantly fewer very small orders (less than 100 members) are included in the latter sample. This underrepresentation and its implications have been discussed in chapter four. Regarding rate of master's degrees, the medians for the two samples are very similar; however, the means differ significantly, as do standard deviations. This points up the fact that in the larger sample there exists greater diversity in educational levels than in the smaller sample. In all probability, the differences in size of orders included in the samples explain the differences in means since small orders, on the whole, are less educated than larger orders. Excluding the very small orders in the smaller sample means that less diversity in educational rates would result.

The two samples are very similar on both the change measure and rates of leaving. In fact, on both measures, the medians differ by only one-tenth of one percent. Since change and rate of leaving are central variables throughout the study, the close approximation of the two samples is very important.

4. Comparison of Sample to Total Population

The mail survey was sent to presidents or provincial superiors of religious orders of women in the United States. A mailing list was supplied by the Conference of Major Superiors of Women (CMSW), a national organization whose membership consists of the presidents of religious orders and provincial superiors. The CMSW is a national organization for leadership in religious orders. While every major administrator of active religious orders is invited and encouraged to belong to the organization, there are 144 orders whose administrators do not belong. Since the CMSW membership mailing list was used in the present study,. these 144 orders are excluded from the study. A comparison of these orders with the 430 that did receive a questionnaire is possible by using data compiled in the *Official Catholic Directory*, a resource report compiled annually on statistics for the Catholic Church in the United States.

Inclusion in the *Official Catholic Directory* is voluntary in that religious orders are asked to send in an annual report of current statistics, but no pressure can be brought to bear upon orders that do not comply. While the majority of orders in the United States are officially listed in the *Directory*, there are some that are not. Of the 430 orders that were included in the CMSW mailing list, 58 were not listed in the *Directory*. Of these 58 orders, 39 responded to the survey and 19 did not. The use of the *Official Catholic Directory*, therefore, to compare orders that received the questionnaire and those that did not and also to compare respondents and nonrespondents is not ideal in that the mailing list used and the listing in the *Directory* are not isomorphic. However, it is the only source available giving organizational data for religious orders on a national basis. The fact that 87% of the orders receiving questionnaires are listed in the *Directory* assures a reasonably accurate picture of the characteristics of the population included in the survey and of the representativeness of the orders that did respond.

Population Characteristics: Comparison of Orders Receiving Questionnaire with Those That Did Not Receive Questionnaire

In general, orders that do not belong to CMSW and therefore did not receive a questionnaire are small orders with motherhouses outside the United States. Of the 251 orders with motherhouses in the United States, only 27 do not belong to CMSW. On the other hand, 108 of the 237 with motherhouses outside the United States, or 45%, were included in the CMSW mailing list. There are 129 orders with foreign motherhouses that did receive the questionnaire; however, this is just slightly over half of all the orders in the United States. There is, therefore, some underrepresentation in the present study of orders with foreign motherhouses. However, statistical analyses regarding rates of leaving showed no significant relationship between location of motherhouses and the phenomenon of leaving.

There is also in the population studied an underrepresentation of orders with fewer than 100 members. Eighty-eight orders or 61% of those not included in the study have less than 100 members. There are, however, 53 orders with fewer than 100 members that are included among respondents so that it is possible to study trends in small orders even though such orders are underrepresented in the present research.

Regarding year orders were founded and year of first foundation in the United States, there are no systematic biases in the population that did not receive a questionnaire. One hundred and twenty of the orders not included in the survey reported no data on location in the United States of administrative headquarters so it is impossible to estimate representativeness of geographical location.

Population Characteristics: Comparison of Orders That Responded to Questionnaire with Those That Did Not Respond

When orders that responded to the questionnaire are compared with orders that received a questionnaire but did not respond, there are several patterns that are evident. Of the 95 orders with a membership under 100, 53 orders or 55% responded to the survey while 30 orders or 80% of those with a membership over 1,000 responded. There is, therefore, underrepresentation of small orders in the survey data. Since a significant number of small orders did respond, it is still possible to perform meaningful statistical analyses of characteristics relating to size of orders. There is no way of determining why small orders did not respond. However, because of limited personnel, some small orders do not have a full-time secretary or record keeper, and it is possible that detailed organizational data were not available.

Regarding country of motherhouse, there is no significant bias among the orders that responded. Orders with motherhouses in the United States are somewhat overrepresented compared with orders having motherhouses in foreign countries. One hundred and sixty-five orders or 73% of all those that received a survey have central headquarters in the United States. However, among the respondents there are orders with motherhouses in a variety of countries, so that comparability on this variable is possible.

Every region in the United States is represented in the survey. There are no differences in patterns of response for any of the regions, so that every area of the United States is represented approximately evenly in the survey. The same is true when year of founding and year of first foundation in the United States are compared for respondents and nonrespondents. In general, then, the only significant underrepresentation in the survey is on the part of orders with fewer than 100 members.

Notes

Preface

1. Robert K. Merton, "Insiders and Outsiders: A Chapter in the Sociology of Knowledge," *American Journal of Sociology* 78 (July 1972): 9–47.
2. Leon Joseph Cardinal Suenens, *The Nun in the World*.

Introduction

1. Kathryn Hulme, *The Nun's Story*.
2. Amitai Etzioni, *A Comparative Analysis of Complex Organizations*.

1. Religious Orders: Old and New

1. *Acta et Documenta Congressus Internationales Superiorissum Generalium*, p. 303.
2. Sister Bertrand Meyers, D.C., *Sisters for the Twenty-First Century*, p. 129.
3. For a detailed discussion of the Sister Formation Movement, see the *Sister Formation Bulletin*, published monthly since 1953 out of the National Sister Formation Office, 2158 Florida Avenue, N.W. Washington, D.C. 20008. For a review of the movement see Meyers, *Sisters for the Twenty-First Century*, pp. 104–124.
4. *Official Catholic Directory*, 1945–1965.
5. "Decree on the Appropriate Renewal of the Religious Life," in *The Documents of Vatican II*, ed. Walter M. Abbot, S.J.
6. R. F. Smith, "Religious Life," in *The New Catholic Encyclopedia*, pp. 287–294.
7. Ibid.
8. Ibid., p. 290.
9. Suzanne Cita-Malard, *Religious Orders of Women*, p. 14.
10. Technically, religious institutes with simple vows are called *congregations* to distinguish them from religious *orders* in which members take solemn vows. In the present study the terms *congregations* and *orders* are used interchangeably according to common usage today. So also the terms *sister* and *nun* are not distinguished, although sisters technically are members of congregations and nuns are members of orders.
11. For further discussion on the immigrant roots of the American Catholic church, see Will Herberg, *Protestant, Catholic, Jew*.
12. John Cogley, *Catholic America*, p. 79.
13. Robert Jay Lifton, *Thought Reform and the Psychology of Totalism*.
14. Ibid., p. 419.

15. George Sorel, *Reflections on Violence*, trans. T. E. Hulme.
16. For a detailed discussion of the concept of consensual validation, see Peter L. Berger, *A Rumor of Angels*.
17. Dom Columba Marmion, *Christ, the Life of the Soul*, p. 52.
18. Thomas à Kempis, *The Imitation of Christ*, p. 130.
19. Ibid., p. 191.
20. Marmion, *Christ, the Life of the Soul*, p. 61.
21. Benjamin Zablocki, *The Joyful Community*, pp. 27–33.
22. Berger, *A Rumor of Angels*.
23. Erving Goffman, *Asylums*, p. 14.
24. Lifton, *Thought Reform*, p. 422.
25. Ibid., p. 423.
26. Emile Durkheim, *The Elementary Forms of Religious Life*.
27. Lifton, *Thought Reform*, p. 425.
28. Ibid., p. 427.
29. Ibid., p. 429.
30. Ibid., p. 430.
31. Ibid., p. 433.
32. Emile Durkheim, *The Division of Labor in Society*, trans. George Simpson.

2. Sociological Perspectives

1. Benjamin Zablocki, *The Joyful Community*, p. 19.
2. Jesse R. Pitts, "On Communes," *Contemporary Sociology* 2, no. 4 (July 1973): 351–359, quotation on p. 351.
3. Maren Lockwood Carden, *Oneida*, p. xvi.
4. Ernst Troeltsch, *The Social Teachings of the Christian Churches*, 1: 331–335.
5. Hulme, *The Nun's Story*. The book was also produced as a movie and has been shown frequently on television.
6. Rosabeth Moss Kanter, *Commitment and Community*, p. 169.
7. Robert K. Merton, "The Role-Set: Problems in Sociological Theory," *British Journal of Sociology* 8 (1956): 106–118.
8. Lewis A. Coser, *Greedy Institutions*, p. 139.
9. Georg Simmel, *Conflict and the Web of Group Affiliations*, trans. Kurt H. Wolff and Reinhard Bendix, p. 150.
10. Philip E. Slater, "On Social Regression," *American Sociological Review* 28 (June 1963): 339–364.
11. Coser, *Greedy Institutions*, p. 139.
12. Yonina Talmon, *Family and Community in the Kibbutz*, pp. 143–150.
13. Coser, *Greedy Institutions*, pp. 154–155.
14. Talmon, *Family and Community*, p. 151.
15. Kanter, *Commitment and Community*, pp. 63–64.
16. Goffman, *Asylums*, pp. 4–5.
17. John Lofland, *Doomsday Cult*.
18. Amitai Etzioni, *A Comparative Analysis of Complex Organizations*.
19. Robert K. Merton and Alice S. Rossi, "Contributions to the Theory of Reference Group Behavior," in *Social Theory and Social Structure*, p. 287.
20. Robert K. Merton, "Continuities in the Theory of Reference Groups and Social Structure," in *Social Theory and Social Structure*, p. 339.

21. Carden, *Oneida*, pp. 91–94.
22. Goffman, *Asylums*, p. 111.
23. For a discussion of the voluntary organization model see David L. Sills, *The Volunteers*, pp. 253–268.
24. Gillian Lindt Gollin, *Moravians in Two Worlds*.
25. For a discussion of the types of contextual data and its uses in research, see Paul F. Lazarsfeld and Herbert Menzel, "On the Relation between Individual and Collective Properties," in *A Sociological Reader on Complex Organizations*, ed. Amitai Etzioni, pp. 499–516.
26. CARA is a research organization supported by the American Catholic bishops as well as by contracted research projects. The goal of the organization is to conduct research on religiously oriented topics, especially those with policy implications.
27. A questionnaire was sent to every order of active religious women in the United States that had membership in the Conference of Major Superiors of Women. When this list is compared with the *Official Catholic Directory*, 144 orders are excluded. Most of these orders are very small in size of membership and have motherhouses outside the United States.
28. Systematic comparisons on numerous demographic variables were made between orders that responded and those that did not respond by utilizing data from the *Official Catholic Directory*. Overall there are no significant differences in the two groups. While there is a slight underrepresentation of small orders among the respondents, sufficient small orders did respond to make statistical analysis on size meaningful.
29. The title Conference of Major Superiors of Women has been changed to the National Leadership Conference since the survey was sent.
30. For a discussion of why some orders responded to the council's decree on change more rapidly than other orders, see Marie Augusta Neal, S.N.D. "The Relation between Religious Belief and Structural Change in Religious Orders: Developing an Effective Measuring Instrument," *Review of Religious Research* 12, no. 1 (Fall 1970): 2–16. Also, Marie Augusta Neal, S.N.D., "A Theoretical Analysis of Renewal in Religious Orders in the U.S.A.," *Social Compass* 18, no. 1 (1971): 7–25.

3. Declining Membership in Religious Orders

1. *Acta et Documenta Congressus Internationales Superiorissum Generalium*, p. 333.
2. Kanter, *Commitment and Community*, pp. 76–91.
3. Carden, *Oneida*.
4. Gollin, *Moravians in Two Worlds*.

4. Education and the Exodus

1. Kanter, *Commitment and Community*.
2. Gollin, *Moravians in Two Worlds*, p. 150.
3. Milford E. Spiro, *Kibbutz*, p. 206.
4. Talmon, *Family and Community*.
5. The cutting point for defining what constitutes a small and a large order is basically self-definition on the part of orders themselves. In the course of conducting research and serving as a consultant in religious orders, it became evident that there exists

among orders an implicit definition of size categories. For example, in one instance, a particular order lost approximately 100 members over a three-year span. The result was that membership dropped from about 400 members to 300. In describing the order, one of the administrators stressed the fact that the order, therefore, could no longer be considered a large order but was now numbered among the small orders in the country. In the same vein, in the course of conducting one of the case studies for the present research, the remark was made that the order was among the large orders in the United States since it had over 1,000 members. Therefore, size is not simply an arbitrary categorization but has a perceptual basis within the orders themselves.

6. Durkheim, *The Division of Labor*, pp. 256–266.
7. Peter M. Blau, *The Organization of Academic Work*, pp. 49–57.
8. Durkheim, *The Division of Labor*, p. 131.

5. Why the Exodus from Religious Orders?

1. Zablocki, *The Joyful Community*.
2. John A. Hostetler, *Amish Society*.
3. Merton, ''Insiders and Outsiders,'' pp. 9–47.
4. Charles Kadushiñ, ''Reason Analysis,'' in *The New International Encyclopedia for the Social Sciences*, pp. 338–342.
5. Ibid.

6. Convents: Reflections on Their Present and Future

1. Robert K. Merton, ''The Unanticipated Consequences of Purposive Social Action,'' *American Sociological Review* 1 (December 1936): 894–904.
2. *Official Catholic Directory*, 1950–1975.
3. Robert K. Merton, ''Bureaucratic Structure and Personality,'' in *Social Theory and Social Structure*, p. 253.

Bibliography

Unpublished Material

Bluth, Elizabeth Jean. "A Convent without Walls: A Case Study in Sociological Innovation." Ph.D. dissertation, University of California, 1969.

Gannon, Thomas M., S.J. "The Organization of Religious Professionals." Ph.D. dissertation, University of Chicago, 1972.

Molitor, Sister M. Margaret Anne. "A Comparative Study of Dropouts and Nondropouts in a Religious Community." Ph.D. dissertation, Catholic University of America, 1967.

Oliss, Sister Patricia Ann. "Beliefs, Behavioral Norms and Commitment in Four Religious Orders." M.A. thesis, Wayne State University, 1971.

Books and Articles

Abbot, Walter M., S.J., ed. *The Documents of Vatican II*. New York: America Press, 1966.

Abrams, Philip, and Andrew McCulloch. *Communes, Sociology, and Society*. New York: Cambridge University Press, 1976.

Abramson, E.; H. A. Cutler; A. W. Kautz; and M. Mendelson. "Social Power and Commitment: A Theoretical Statement." *American Sociological Review* 23 (February 1958): 15–22.

Acta et Documenta Congressus Internationales Superiorissum Generalium. Rome: Editiones Paulinae, 1952.

Argyris, Chris. *Integrating the Individual and the Organization*. New York: John Wiley & Sons, 1964.

Baldwin, Monica. *I Leap Over the Wall*. New York: Rinehart & Co., 1950.

Barrett, Jon H. *Individual Goals and Organizational Objectives: A Study of Integration Mechanisms*. Ann Arbor: University of Michigan, Institute for Social Research, 1970.

Bartlett, Laile E. *The Vanishing Parson*. Boston: Beacon Press, 1971.

Barton, Allen. "Organizations: Methods of Research." In *The New International Encyclopedia of the Social Sciences*. Vol. 2, pp. 334–341. New York: Macmillan Co. and Free Press, 1968.

Becker, Howard S. "Notes on the Concept of Commitment." *American Journal of Sociology* 66 (July 1960): 32–40.

Bendix, Reinhardt. *Max Weber: An Intellectual Portrait*. Garden City, N.Y.: Doubleday, 1960.

Bennett, John W. *Hutterian Brethren: The Agricultural Economy and Social Organization of a Communal People*. Stanford: Stanford University Press, 1967.

Bennis, Warren, and Philip E. Slater. *The Temporary Society*. New York: Harper and Row, 1968.

Berger, Peter L. *A Rumor of Angels: Modern Society and the Rediscovery of the Supernatural*. Garden City, N.Y.: Doubleday, 1969.

———. *The Sacred Canopy: Elements of a Sociological Theory of Religion*. Garden City, N.Y.: Doubleday, 1969.

Bettelheim, Bruno. *The Informed Heart*. Glencoe, Ill.: Free Press, 1960.

Birnbaum, Z. W., and Monroe G. Sirken. "Bias Due to Nonavailability in Sampling Surveys." *Journal of the American Statistical Association* 45 (1950): 98–110.

Blau, Peter M. *Exchange and Power in Social Life*. New York: John Wiley & Sons, 1964.

———. *The Organization of Academic Work*. New York: John Wiley & Sons, 1973.

———, and W. Richard Scott. *Formal Organizations: A Comparative Approach*. San Francisco: Chandler, 1962.

Boguslaw, Robert. *The New Utopians: A Study of System Design and Social Change*. Englewood Cliffs, N.J.: Prentice-Hall, 1965.

Brim, Orville G., Jr. "Adult Socialization." In *Socialization and Society*, edited by John A. Clausen, pp. 192–226. Boston: Little, Brown & Co., 1968.

Caplow, Theodore. *Principles of Organization*. New York: Harcourt, Brace & World, 1964.

Carden, Maren Lockwood. *Oneida: Utopian Community to Modern Corporation*. Baltimore: Johns Hopkins Press, 1969.

Chafee, G. "Isolated Sects as an Object for Research." *American Journal of Sociology* 35 (1958): 618–630.

Cita-Malard, Suzanne. *Religious Orders of Women*. New York: Hawthorn Books, 1964.

Clark, Burton R. "Organizational Adaptation and Precarious Values." *American Sociological Review* 21 (June 1956): 327–336.

Clausen, John A., and Robert N. Ford. "Controlling Bias in Mail Questionnaires." *Journal of the American Statistical Association* 42 (1947): 497–511.

Cogley, John. *Catholic America*. New York: Dial Press, 1973.

Cohen, Ely. *Human Behavior in the Concentration Camps*. London: Jonathan Cape, 1954.

Conkin, Paul K. *Two Paths to Utopia: The Hutterites and the Llano Colony*. Lincoln: University of Nebraska Press, 1965.

Coser, Lewis A. *The Functions of Social Conflict*. New York: Free Press, 1964.

———. *Greedy Institutions: Patterns of Undivided Commitment*. New York: Free Press, 1974.

———. "Sects and Sectarians." *Dissent* 1 (Autumn 1954): 360–369.

Cross, Robert D. *The Emergence of Liberal Catholicism in America*. Cambridge, Mass.: Harvard University Press, 1958.

Cryns, Arthur G. "Dogmatism of Catholic Clergy and Ex-Clergy: A Study of Ministerial Role Perseverance and Open-Mindedness." *Journal for the Scientific Study of Religion* 9 (Fall 1970): 239–243.

Demerath, N. J., and Victor Thiessen. "On Spitting against the Wind: Organizational Precariousness and American Irreligion." *American Journal of Sociology* 71 (May 1966): 674–687.

Deming, W. Edwards. "On a Probability Mechanism to Attain an Economic Balance between the Resultant Response and the Bias of Nonresponse." *Journal of the American Statistical Association* 48 (1953): 743–772.

Durkheim, Emile. *The Division of Labor in Society*. Translated by George Simpson. New York: Free Press, 1966. 1st ed., 1933.

———. *The Elementary Forms of Religious Life*. New York: Free Press, 1965.

———. *Suicide*. Glencoe, Ill.: Free Press, 1951.

Ellis, John Tracey. *American Catholicism*. Chicago: University of Chicago Press, 1969.

Etzioni, Amitai. *A Comparative Analysis of Complex Organizations*. New York: Free Press, 1961.

———. "Functional Differentiation of Elites." *American Journal of Sociology* 64 (1959): 476–487.

———. "Solidaric Work-Groups in Collective Settlements." *Human Organization* 16 (1957): 2–6.

Festinger, Leon. *When Prophecy Fails*. New York: Harper & Row, 1956.

Fichter, Joseph H. *America's Forgotten Priests*. New York: Harper & Row, 1968.

———. *Religion as an Occupation*. Notre Dame: University of Notre Dame Press, 1961.

Francis, E. K. "Toward a Typology of Religious Orders." *American Journal of Sociology* 55 (1950): 437–449.

Gannon, Thomas M., S.J. "Priest/Minister: Profession or Nonprofession." *Review of Religious Research* 12 (1971): 66–79.

———, and George W. Traub, S.J. *The Desert and the City: An Interpretation of the History of Christian Spirituality*. London: Macmillan & Co., 1969.

Gerth, H. H., and C. Wright Mills. *From Max Weber: Essays in Sociology*. New York: Oxford University Press, 1958.

Goffman, Erving. *Asylums*. Garden City, N.Y.: Doubleday, 1961.

Gollin, Gillian Lindt. *Moravians in Two Worlds: A Study of Changing Communities*. New York: Columbia University Press, 1967.

Goode, William. *After Divorce*. Glencoe, Ill.: Free Press, 1956.

Gouldner, Alvin W. "The Norm of Reciprocity: A Preliminary Statement." *American Sociological Review* 25 (April 1960): 161–179.

Gouldner, Helen P. "Dimensions of Organizational Commitment." *Administrative Science Quarterly* 4 (December 1960): 468–487.

Greely, Andrew M., S.J.; William C. McCready; and Kathleen McCourt. *Catholic Schools in a Declining Church*. Kansas City: Sheed & Ward, 1976.

Griffin, Mary. *The Courage to Choose: An American Nun's Story*. Boston: Little, Brown & Co., 1975.

Gross, Neal, and William E. Martin. "On Group Cohesiveness." *American Journal of Sociology* 57 (May 1952): 546–564.

Hadden, Jeffrey K. *The Gathering Storm in the Churches*. Garden City, N.Y.: Doubleday, 1969.

———, ed. *Religion in Radical Transition*. New Brunswick, N.J.: Transaction Books, Rutgers State University, 1971.

Hall, Douglas T., and Benjamin Schneider. *Organizational Climates and Careers: The Work Lives of Priests*. New York: Seminar Press, 1973.

Hedgepeth, William, and Dennis Stock. *The Alternative: Communal Life in New America*. New York: Macmillan Co., 1970.

Henricks, Walter A. "Adjustments for Bias by Non-response in Mailed Surveys." *Agricultural Economic Research* 1 (1949): 52–56.

Herberg, Will. *Protestant, Catholic, Jew*. Garden City, N.Y.: Doubleday, 1955.

Hobsbawm, E. J. *Primitive Rebels: Studies in Archaic Forms of Social Movement in the 19th and 20th Centuries*. Manchester, England: Manchester University Press, 1959.

Hostetler, John A. *Amish Society*. Baltimore: Johns Hopkins Press, 1963.

Hulme, Kathryn. *The Nun's Story*. Boston: Little, Brown & Co., 1956.

Huxley, Aldous. *Brave New World and Brave New World Revisited*. New York: Harper & Row, 1965.

Infield, Henrik F. *Utopia and Experiment: Essays in the Sociology of Cooperation*. New York: Praeger, 1955.

Jacobs, Ruth Harriet. "Emotive and Control Groups as Mutated New American Utopian Communities." *Journal of Applied Behavioral Science* 7 (March–April 1971): 234–251.

Johnson, Benton. "On Church and Sect." *American Sociological Review* 38 (1963): 539–549.

Jones, Maxwell. *The Therapeutic Community*. New York: Basic Books, 1965.

Jud, Gerald J.; Edgar W. Mills, Jr.; and Genevieve Walters Burch. *Ex-Pastors: Why Men Leave the Parish Ministry*. Philadelphia: Pilgrim Press, 1970.

Kadushin, Charles. "Reason Analysis." In *The New International Encyclopedia for the Social Sciences*. Vol. 13, pp. 338–342. New York: Macmillan Co. and Free Press, 1968.

———. *Why People Go to Psychiatrists*. New York: Atherton Press, 1969.

Kanter, Rosabeth Moss. *Commitment and Community: Communes and Utopias in Sociological Perspective*. Cambridge, Mass.: Harvard University Press, 1972.

———. "Commitment and Social Organization: A Study of Commitment Mechanisms in Utopian Communities." *American Sociological Review* 33 (August 1968): 499–517.

———. *Communes: Creating and Managing the Collective Life*. New York: Harper & Row, 1973.

———. "Communes." *Psychology Today* 4 (July 1970): 56–70.

Katz, Daniel. "The Motivational Basis of Organizational Behavior." *Behavioral Science* 9 (April 1964): 131–146.

———, and Robert L. Kahn. *The Social Psychology of Organizations*. New York: John Wiley & Sons, 1966.

Kelman, Herbert C. "Compliance, Identification, and Internalization: Three Processes of Attitude Change." *Journal of Conflict Resolution* 2 (March 1958): 51–60.

Kempis, Thomas à. *The Imitation of Christ*. London: Burns, Oates, & Washbourne, 1925.

Lazarsfeld, Paul F., and Herbert Menzel. "On the Relation between Individual and Collective Properties." In *A Sociological Reader on Complex Organizations*, edited by Amitai Etzioni, pp. 499–516. New York: Holt, Rinehart & Winston, 1969.

Lazarsfeld, Paul F., and M. Rosenberg, eds. *The Language of Social Research*. Glencoe, Ill.: Free Press, 1955.

Lifton, Robert Jay. *Thought Reform and the Psychology of Totalism*. New York: Norton, 1961.

Lockwood, Maren. "The Experimental Utopia in America." *Daedalus* 94 (Spring 1965): 401–418.

Lofland, John. *Doomsday Cult: A Study of Conversion, Proselytization, and Maintenance of Faith*. Englewood Cliffs, N.J.: Prentice-Hall, 1966.

————, and Rodney Stark. "Becoming a World-Saver: A Theory of Conversion to a Deviant Perspective." *American Sociological Review* 30 (December 1965): 362–875.

Loomis, Charles P. *Social Systems: Essays on Their Persistence and Change*. Princeton, N.J.: D. Van Nostrand, 1960.

Luckmann, Thomas. *The Invisible Religion*. London: Collier Macmillan, 1967.

Mannheim, Karl. *Ideology and Utopia: An Introduction to the Sociology of Knowledge*. Translated by Louis Wirth and Edward Shils. New York: Harcourt, Brace & World, 1936.

Manuel, Frank E., ed. *Utopias and Utopian Thought*. Boston: Houghton Mifflin, 1966.

Marmion, Dom Columba. *Christ, the Life of the Soul*. St. Louis, Mo.: B. Herder Book Co., 1925.

Mayntz, Renate. "Role Distance, Role Identification, and Amoral Role Behavior." *European Journal of Sociology* 11 (November 1970): 368–378.

Meadows, Paul. "Movements of Social Withdrawal." *Sociology and Social Research* 29 (September–October 1944): 46–50.

Merton, Robert K. "Bureaucratic Structure and Personality" and "Continuities in the Theory of Reference Groups and Social Structure." In *Social Theory and Social Structure*. Enl. ed. New York: Free Press, 1968.

————. "Insiders and Outsiders: A Chapter in the Sociology of Knowledge." *American Journal of Sociology* 78 (July 1972): 9–47.

————. "The Role-Set: Problems in Sociological Theory." *British Journal of Sociology* 8 (1956): 106–118.

————. "The Unanticipated Consequences of Purposive Social Action." *American Sociological Review* 1 (December 1936): 894–904.

————, and Alice S. Rossi. "Contributions to the Theory of Reference Group Behavior." In *Social Theory and Social Structure*. Enl. ed. New York: Free Press, 1968.

Messinger, Sheldon L. "Organizational Transformation: A Case Study of a Declining Social Movement." *American Sociological Review* 20 (January 1955): 3–10.

Meyers, Sister Bertrand, D.C. *Sisters for the Twenty-First Century*. New York: Sheed & Ward, 1965.

Moore, Wilbert E. "The Utility of Utopias." *American Sociological Review* 31 (December 1966): 765–772.

Muckenhirn, Sister M. Charles Borromeo, E.S.C., ed. *The Changing Sister*. Notre Dame, Ind.: Fides Press, 1965.

————. *The New Nuns*. New York: New American Library, 1967.

Murphy, Sister Roseanne. "Organizational Stance and Change: A Comparative Study of Three Religious Communities." *Review of Religious Research* (Fall 1966): 37–50.

Neal, Marie Augusta, S.N.D. "The Relation between Religious Belief and Structural Change in Religious Orders: Developing an Effective Measuring Instrument." *Review of Religious Research* 12, no. 1 (Fall 1970): 2–16.

————. "The Relation between Religious Belief and Structural Change in Religious Orders: Some Evidence." *Review of Religious Research* 12 (Spring 1971): 153–164.

————. "A Theoretical Analysis of Renewal in Religious Orders in the U.S.A." *Social Compass* 18, no. 1 (1971): 7–25.

————. *Values and Interests in Social Change*. Englewood Cliffs, N.J.: Prentice-Hall, 1965.

Nie, N. H.; D. H. Bent; and C. H. Hull. *Statistical Package for the Social Sciences*. New York: McGraw-Hill, 1970.

Niebuhr, H. Richard. *The Social Sources of Denominationalism*. Cleveland and New York: World Publishing Co., 1957.

O'Dea, Thomas F. *The Catholic Crisis*. Boston: Beacon Press, 1968.

———. "Five Paradoxes of Institutionalization." In *Sociological Theory, Values, and Sociocultural Change*, edited by Edward A. Tiriyakian. New York: Harper and Row, 1963.

———. *The Sociology of Religion*. Englewood Cliffs, N.J.: Prentice-Hall, 1966.

Official Catholic Directory. New York: P. J. Kennedy & Sons, 1940–1976.

Otto, Rudolf. *The Idea of the Holy*. New York: Oxford University Press, 1958.

Parsons, Talcott. *The Social System*. Glencoe, Ill.: Free Press, 1951.

———. *Societies: Evolutionary and Comparative Perspectives*. Englewood Cliffs, N.J.: Prentice-Hall, 1966.

Pfautz, Harold. "The Sociology of Secularization." *American Journal of Sociology* 61 (September 1955): 121–128.

Pitts, Jesse R. "On Communes." *Contemporary Sociology* 2, no. 4 (July 1973): 351–359.

Pugh, D. C.; David J. Hickson; C. R. Hinings; and C. Turner. "The Context of Organization Structures." *Administrative Science Quarterly* 14 (March 1969): 91–114.

Ritterband, Paul. "Group Disorders in the Public Schools." *American Sociological Review* 38 (August 1973): 461–467.

———. *Schooling, Jobs and International Migration: Israel in Comparative Perspective*. American Sociological Association, Rose Monograph Series. New York: Cambridge University Press, forthcoming.

Rosenfield, Eva. "Social Stratification in a 'Classless' Society." *American Sociological Review* 16 (1951): 766–774.

Sagarin, Edward. *Odd Man In: Societies of Deviants in America*. Chicago: Quadrangle Books, 1969.

Schallert, Eugene J., and Jacqueline M. Kelley. "Some Factors Associated with Voluntary Withdrawal from the Catholic Priesthood." *Lumen Vitae* 25 (September 1970): 425–460.

Schmalenback, Herman. "The Sociological Category of Communion." In *Theories of Society*, edited by Talcott Parsons et al. Vol. 1. New York: Free Press, 1961.

Schoenherr, Richard A., and Andrew M. Greeley. "Role Commitment Processes and the American Catholic Priesthood." *American Sociological Review* 39 (June 1974): 407–426.

Selznick, Philip. "Foundations of the Theory of Organization." *American Sociological Review* 13 (February 1948): 25–35.

———. *TVA and the Grass Roots*. New York: Harper Torch Books, 1966.

Shils, Edward. "Charisma, Order, and Status." *American Sociological Review* 30 (April 1965): 199–213.

Sills, David L. *The Volunteers*. Glencoe, Ill.: Free Press, 1958.

Simmel, Georg. *Conflict and the Web of Group Affiliations*. Translated by Kurt H. Wolff and Reinhard Bendix. Glencoe, Ill.: Free Press, 1955.

———. *The Sociology of Georg Simmel*. Edited by Kurt H. Wolff. New York: Free Press, 1964.

Simpson, R. L., and W. H. Gupley. "Goals, Environmental Pressures and Organizational Characteristics." *American Sociological Review* 27 (June 1962): 344–351.

Slater, Philip E. *The Pursuit of Loneliness*. Boston: Beacon Press, 1970.
———. "On Social Regression." *American Sociological Review* 28 (June 1963): 339–364.
Smith, R. F. "Religious Life." In *The New Catholic Encyclopedia*, pp. 287–294. New York: McGraw-Hill, 1967.
Sorel, George. *Reflections on Violence*. Translated by T. E. Hulme. New York: Peter Smith Publications, 1941.
Spiro, Melford E. *Kibbutz: Venture in Utopia*. Cambridge, Mass.: Harvard University Press, 1956.
Stephan, Frederick, and Philip J. McCarthy. "Problems of Accessibility and Cooperation." In *Sampling Opinion: An Analysis of Survey Procedures*. New York: John Wiley & Sons, 1958.
Suenens, Cardinal Leon Joseph. *The Nun in the World*. Westminster, Md.: Newman Press, 1962.
Talmon, Yonina. "Aging in Israel: A Planned Society." *American Journal of Sociology* 57 (November 1961): 284–295.
———. *Family and Community in the Kibbutz*. Cambridge, Mass.: Harvard University Press, 1972.
Toennies, Ferdinand. *Community and Society*. Translated by Charles P. Loomis. East Lansing: Michigan State University Press, 1957.
Troeltsch, Ernst. *The Social Teachings of the Christian Churches*. Vol. 1. New York: Macmillan Co., 1931.
Turner, Ralph, and Lewis M. Killian. *Collective Behavior*. Englewood Cliffs, N.J.: Prentice-Hall, 1957.
Udy, Stanley H., Jr. "The Comparative Analysis of Organizations." In *Handbook of Organizations*, edited by James G. March, pp. 678–709. Chicago: Rand McNally, 1965.
Wallace, Anthony F. C. "Revitalization Movements." *American Anthropologist* 58 (April 1956): 264–281.
Wallace, Samuel E., ed. *Total Institutions*. Chicago: Aldine Publishing Co., 1971. [Essays originally appeared in *Transaction Magazine*.]
Webber, Everett. *Escape to Utopia: The Communal Movement in America*. New York: Hastings House, 1958.
Weber, Max. *The Protestant Ethic and the Spirit of Capitalism*. New York: Charles Scribner's Sons, 1958.
———. *The Theory of Social and Economic Organization*. Translated by A. M. Henderson and Talcott Parsons. Glencoe, Ill.: Free Press, 1947.
Whitney, Norman. *Experiments in Community*. Wallingford, Pa.: Pendle Hill, 1966.
Wilson, Bryan R. "An Analysis of Sect Development." *American Sociological Review* 24 (February 1959): 1–15.
Yablonsky, Lewis. *Synanon: The Tunnel Back*. New York: Macmillan Co., 1965.
Yinger, J. Milton. "Contraculture and Subculture." *American Sociological Review* 25 (October 1960): 625–635.
Yuchtman, Ephraim. "Reward Distribution and Work-Role Attractiveness in the Kibbutz—Reflections on Equity Theory." *American Sociological Review* 37 (October 1972): 581–595.
Zablocki, Benjamin. *The Joyful Community*. Baltimore: Penguin, 1971.